# BLESSED BUT BROKE

## THE 60-DAY BIBLICAL FINANCE GUIDE TO SAVE MONEY, BUILD WEALTH AND CHOOSE WISDOM

Darryl Boyles

Editor: Tempestt Johnson

Book Cover Design: Melvin McClanahan Jr. of Artistic Expressions

Printed in the United States of America.

 Published by Bridge the Gap.

All definitions, unless otherwise indicated, are used from the Merriam-Webster Dictionary; Merriam-Webster.com. 2021.

Dear Reader,

I wrote this book for people who are saved and struggling financially.

There's a pandemic of Christians who are living in or too close to poverty. I know because I've been there. I remember going to church faithfully quoting that I was the "lender, not the borrower" and that "God shall supply all my needs." I confessed overflow yet my bank account was steadily overdrawn, and my bills were still past due. If you're anything like me, you're tired of being broke. You're fed up with worrying about how your bills are going to get paid or wondering when you'll have enough money to do the things you enjoy.

I was paying my tithes consistently but still living paycheck-to-paycheck. I wondered if there was an unresolved problem in my life blocking my financial increase. Then, I realized my prayers and verbal confessions didn't match how I managed my money. I prayed for a "financial overflow," but I wasn't saving; I spent every dollar I earned; and I didn't have a real plan for my money.

I began to go to the Bible for answers, and the principles I learned changed my relationship with money. This book was created to give you fresh revelations and information to improve your finances.

Money itself isn't evil; however, the lack of money can lead people to do things that are not of God. In this book, you will spend sixty days learning biblical and practical principles that you can apply to your finances starting today. Educating yourself in the area of finances will lead you to overflow much quicker than complaining.

Don't delay! There's no time like the present to turn your finances and life around. Don't wait until you're facing an eviction, bankruptcy, repossession, or even divorce before you begin to change your money story. You can choose to break the paycheck-to-paycheck cycle now. I'm ready to go on this journey with you.

**Download your FREE Quick start Guide - 5 Ways to Make Your Paycheck Stretch.**

I would like to offer you a free quick start guide to help you get on the road to financial freedom. It's called "5 Ways to Make Your Paycheck Stretch: Even If Money Is Tight Right Now."

Go to **ImBreakingTheCycle.com** to download it right now as my free gift to you.

Thanks for taking the time to read this devotional. Here's to your fresh start!

Darryl

# ACKNOWLEDGEMENTS

To my beautiful wife Kiosha: thank you for being a part of my life. So many of my accomplishments are because of you. When I feel down, you encourage me. When I am unsure of myself, you affirm me. When I feel stuck, you help me grow. You've truly made every area of my life better.

To my phenomenal kids: being a Dad is one of the most vital roles I could ever have. To my daughter Noelle and my son Grayson: it's my prayer that you two would walk in abundance all the days of your lives and in every area of your lives.

To Marcus R. Shiver: thank you for being the Man of God I needed at just the right time. I grew up in church, but you were the first one to really Pastor me. You taught me the Word of God and how to make it come alive in my life. Away from church, you mentored and educated me on proper manhood. It's because of men like you that boys develop into men. Thanks for allowing God to use you.

To Ricardo Palmer: thank you for always being there for me when I need you. You have a true gift of giving specific, Godly advice. Your level of knowledge and revelation of the Word of God is something that I aspire to have. I hope I am someday able to be a blessing to you, as you are to me. Thanks for being a mentor and an occasional therapist!

# TABLE OF CONTENTS

# INTRODUCTION

Growing up, I struggled financially. I committed myself to reading every finance and personal development book I could get my hands on and applied those strategies and tips to my life. I improved my credit score, purchased my first home, and built a sizable savings account. After seeing an improvement in my life, I made it my mission to help others reach their personal goals in business, money, and life.

During a session with a client, the subject of faith and finances arose. She stated that either money was talked about too much or not enough in churches. Her statement caused me to reflect on my own upbringing in church. The only thing that came to mind about faith and finances was paying tithes and offering.

For many, the area of faith and finances is a sore spot. I can't tell you how many people I've spoken to who have had to endure heartbreak when it came to money and ministry. They've been a part of churches that have treated tithes and offerings like a Ponzi scheme where public pressure and guilt are used to sway members to give love offerings. They have been members of churches where financial teachings haven't gone beyond the ten percent.

And then there is another group: a group where their church leadership regularly held financial workshops to benefit its members, not just the ministry. This group also has financial counselors readily available for consultations to assist in the improvement of financial conditions. They also host and conduct personal finance workshops and seminars for its members. I personally believe the type of financial teachings in a ministry is based on the leadership's experiences with finances. In my personal experience, church leadership with a healthy relationship with money offers more holistic financial teaching for its members. When the leadership has an unhealthy relationship with money, you will find manipulative practices and/or the lack of financial instruction nearby.

In this devotional book, we will go straight to the source as our guide for financial instruction. The Bible offers many principles in scripture that can be applied to your personal finances that extend beyond tithes and offerings. Commit the next sixty days to the education and application of these biblical principles in order to improve your relationship with money. I pray this book helps to nurture your spiritual growth and challenges you to invite God into new areas of your life.

# DAY 1: CREATE IT

*"In the beginning God created the heavens and the Earth." -Genesis 1:1*

The word; create means to bring something into existence that wasn't there before. As a Christian, you also have the ability to create and bring things into existence. You don't have to settle for your current environment: you were born with the power to change it. If you don't come from a family with a lot of wealth, you're going to have to create wealth for yourself and the next generation. There's nothing wrong with being born into a family with less than ideal financial circumstances. The problem, however, is when every generation is born into financial struggle. You didn't create the poverty within your family, but you have the power to end it. Everyone is already in the process of creating something with his or her finances regardless of the time and energy that's given towards their dollars. You are either proactively creating the financial conditions you want or reactively struggling with the finances you were given. Creating generational wealth will require more time beyond just working a full-time job. Although God had the power to create the heavens and the Earth overnight, He didn't. God was showing us that creating something out of nothing is a process and will require time to complete.

God created the world by speaking things into existence, and this is something of which we have to be very mindful. The words you speak have the power to create your physical reality. This is why I challenge you from this day forward to no longer speak the language of financial struggle. Replace the words, "I can't afford this" with the words, "how can I afford this?" It's not only about the words you speak: it's also about the words you hear that help you with your money. Begin to listen to the conversations of people who are first generation wealth builders. I bet Warren Buffett and Bill Gates don't have arguments over the housewives or who's the GOAT. People with a poverty mindset will invest more time arguing about someone else's money than actually learning about money. Listen to one of the many available podcasts, audiobooks, or YouTube series that educate and inform about finances. Most people who struggle financially weren't educated about finances until they were already adults. Educate yourself and your kid(s) about money as early as possible. The conversations you hear are often repeated, so make sure those words are creating the financial conditions you desire to experience.

As you begin to start your process of building wealth, you're going to have to start with structure. God didn't wait until the Earth was completely filled before He started structuring everything. According to the Merriam-Webster, structure is defined by the ability "to construct or arrange according to a plan; give a plan or organization to." You have to have a plan for your money before you receive it. Every one of your dollars will need a job in a certain aspect of your life. This is what a good budget does. A budget is simply a plan for your money, not a source of restriction. Those who choose not to structure their monies typically don't have very much money. God had a plan for everything He spoke into existence before he created it. God had a plan for the light, darkness, land, waters, birds, and every other living creature. Educate yourself and strategize a plan for each individual dollar that you currently have and all your dollars that are on the way. God is not in the business of wasting resources regardless of how much you pray. God doesn't bless where there's no structure. Stop waiting on the abundance of rain if you haven't even prepared your fields. There will be no overflow until there is organization.

# DAY 2: HAVE DOMINION

*"So God created man in His own image;
in the image of God He created him;
male and female He created them"
-Genesis 1:27*

After God created the environment for human beings to thrive in, He gave us our very first command: the first commandment was for man and woman to be fruitful and multiply (Gen 1:28). God wanted mankind to have dominion, not to be dominated. Living in a constant state of financial hardship places you in a position to be dominated. Money has dominion over you when the majority of the decisions you make are based on the amount of money you have. You have to get into a place financially where the choices you make are what's best for you and your family, not what you can afford. The only time money doesn't matter is when you have it in abundance. When your money is limited so are your options. And when your options are limited, you do what you have to do in order to survive. But, God doesn't want you to just survive: He wants you to be fruitful. Building a life that's based off of living in survival mode will rob you of the experiences that this Earth has to offer. God didn't allow for the creation of traveling the world only for you to be dominated on a job that you hate.

Right after God told us to be fruitful, He established our food supply (Gen. 1:29). This means that food was a priority for God. And your food should also be a priority to you. So much money is wasted on food because of a lack of planning meals. Notice how many drive-thrus are packed on your way to work. Don't be the person who walks past a refrigerator with food inside and a stove that works just to pay someone for food you could have fixed yourself. You could easily spend $20 daily on eating out. At that rate you would spend $7,300 a year on dining out alone because you hate to cook. Eating out can be an expensive habit. Although many spend this money without thought the majority of working adults don't even have $1,000 in savings. When you are in the process of building generational wealth, every dollar matters. Stop flushing your money down the toilet, and put it to work for you instead. Start planning and preparing your meals ahead of schedule in order to avoid that convenient drive thru line. You can't be effective at building wealth when you invest more money in fast food than you do in your assets. Your kid(s) won't be able to benefit financially from all the money you spent on eating out. Start cooking at home and invest the difference saved into cash producing assets.

The money spent on eating can be the difference between poverty and wealth, but the type of food you eat all together can be the difference between a long life and early death. You should strive to reduce and/or eliminate processed foods out of your diet. Some people pray for healing from the same mouth they welcome their illnesses by the foods they choose to eat. If you personally believe eating healthy costs too much, then you have placed too little of a value on your life. High blood pressure, high cholesterol issues, and avoidable diabetes will prevent you from enjoying the wealth you're building. Discipline in your money without discipline in your health will lead to someone else prematurely enjoying your wealth. Along with improving your diet, make the time to exercise. Find an accountability partner to help you improve your health. If you are too busy to workout, try being dead for twenty-four hours out of the day. I challenge you to make the food you eat a priority. Being overweight and having to take medications because of a lack of willpower isn't exercising dominion. Love yourself and your family enough to make the necessary changes to experience a healthy and wealthy life.

# DAY 3: THE CHOICE IS YOURS

*". . .but of the tree of the knowledge of good and evil you shall not eat, for in the day that you eat of it you shall surely die." -Genesis 2:17*

God has finished forming the heavens and the Earth, and He just placed Adam in the Garden of Eden (Gen. 2:8). The Bible teaches us that gold was in the Garden of Eden and the gold of the land was good (Gen. 2:11-12). But somewhere along the line someone convinced people that money was evil. If money were truly evil, God would have told Adam. Money is just a resource that exposes the character of its owner. Building your wealth and being a Christian isn't an either/or option: you can choose to have both. Your treasure is in heaven, but that doesn't mean you should live in poverty here on Earth. The world you live in today is based on money, and the amount you possess will determine the choices you have in life. The level of healthcare, education, housing, nutrition, childcare, and ministry are all based off of the monies that are available. What more could you accomplish in your life if you didn't have to spend 40 plus hours on a job? The amount of wealth you build will be based on the choices you make. Because God is a gentleman, He's given us the power of choice since the very beginning.

When Adam was placed in the Garden of Eden, God told him not to eat of the Tree of the Knowledge of Good and Evil (Gen. 2:17). God didn't force Adam to be obedient: He gave him a choice. God wants your obedience, but He also gives you freewill to make the right choices. Finances aren't different from any other area in your life. Experiencing abundant wealth or financial hardship are both results from choices that you are making with your money. If you want to experience a greater level in your finances, make greater choices with your finances. God doesn't force His way into your finances. You will not be able to build generational wealth regardless of how much you pray if you don't make the right choices with your dollars. Don't pray for money if you're not willing to exercise the discipline to keep it. Choose to focus saving and spending your money on proven assets that will generate more cash flow for you. Cash flow is the amount of cash between your expenses and income that you get to keep. The way you increase your cash flow is to increase your income and decrease your expenses. Some financial gurus would warn you that the real challenge with finances is keeping the money you've made.

I know you work hard for your money: don't make the choice to waste it on things that don't matter. The less money you make, the more disciplined you're going to have to be with your money.

Small money plus good habits will grow your dollars into bigger money. God placed Adam in the Garden to work and tend it (Gen. 2:15). Tend in this context can be defined as to apply oneself. You will have to apply yourself and be an active participant in order to develop your desires into realities. Don't depend on God to perform the work and task that you have the capabilities to do. No one can force you to build generational wealth: it's your choice. Make the choice to save a certain amount of every dollar you make. Make the choice not to jump into debt for luxuries you truly can't afford. Spending money you haven't made yet will limit the financial choices you will have available. Make the choice to develop and stick to a budget with all of your income. Make the choice to improve your credit scores. Make the choice to tithe on a consistent basis. The choices you make with your money today will affect the choices you will have in the future with their money. Use your freewill to create generational wealth.

# DAY 4: COMMUNICATION

*"And He said, 'Who told you that you were naked? Have you eaten from the tree of which I commanded you that you should not eat?'"*
*-Genesis 3:11*

The Garden of Eden was the most perfect situation ever recorded in the Bible. God walked and talked with Adam and Eve on a regular basis, and there weren't any effects of sin nature to deal with. But even in the middle of paradise, there was still adversity to face. What are the conversations that you are having with yourself and others when challenges arise? It's your response to adversity that will be the difference maker. There is never a good time to respond to adversity by taking suggestions from people who seek to do you harm. It was a conversation that led to the downfall of mankind. And it's because of conversations that so many people remain down. The serpent challenged what Eve was instructed to do and convinced her to eat of the Tree of the Knowledge of Good and Evil (Gen. 3:2-6). After she ate of the tree, she gave it to her husband to eat (Gen. 3:6). And then they realized that they were naked and decided to cover themselves using fig leaves (Gen. 3:7). Once confronted, Adam told God that they hid because they were naked. And God responded by saying, "Who told you that you were naked?" (Gen. 3:11).

The information you have about your finances was learned from someone else. Who are you talking to and listening to about money? How are you allowing those conversations to influence you? What did they tell you about finances? Did they say something like, "that's what you work hard for, go ahead and enjoy that money." Or what about this: "You can't take that money with you, might as well enjoy it now." Do you tell yourself this one, "I can afford the payments?" Outside of purchasing a house, if you could truly afford something you wouldn't have to borrow to get it. Do you communicate to yourself that you don't make enough to save and so you save absolutely nothing? If we are to change our finances, we are going to have to change our communication about finances. Instead of saying "I don't make enough," replace it with "how can I make more money"? The conversations with those close to or in poverty in many cases are centered on how to spend their money. Start listening to people who are first generational wealth builders who come from backgrounds similar to yours. The conversations that are being had with people who are building wealth are different.

Before you can change your finances, you must change the communication you are hearing about finances from the correct sources. Don't allow people or your environment to continue to communicate to you that struggling is normal. I challenge you to continue to learn more concerning the area of finances: listen to sermons, attend workshops, study the Word, and let these avenues communicate a different money story to you. You must learn to qualify the people from whom you take financial advice. The serpent wanted the fall of mankind. Ask yourself, what is the motive of this person telling me this? Carefully select and only take advice from people who are headed in the right direction financially and also have your best interest at heart. Remember that the serpent influenced Eve, and Eve influenced Adam to eat of the tree. Who's influencing you in the area of your finances? Who's a part of your life right now that's influencing you to use your current finances to build generational wealth? We need these types of people in our circle on a consistent basis. It's easy to find someone to help you spend your money but not as easy to have someone that will influence you to save and build wealth.

# DAY 5: CAN YOU STAND THE RAIN?

*"Go out of the ark, you and your wife, and your sons, and your sons wives with you" -Genesis 8:16*

Just like Noah built an Ark to withstand the flood waters that were coming, you are going to have to build your finances to be able to withstand the economic hardships of life. What would happen to your household if you lost your job? What would you do if your HVAC unit went out in your house? What would happen if the transmission goes out on your vehicle? What would happen if a natural disaster caused you to evacuate your home? These are all hardships that are bound to happen, so what are you doing to prepare for them? The Bible teaches us that Noah lived differently than everyone else in his generation. This is the same principle you need to apply in your personal finances: living differently. We as Christians are called to be good stewards of our resources and prepare in advance for these hardships. Noah constructed each compartment of the boat so that it would still float. What are the areas of your finances that you are constructing? How much are you putting in personal savings? How much is going toward paying off debt? How much time are you dedicating to creating additional income?

Noah didn't come from a genealogy of ship builders and hadn't even seen rain before. The fact that you haven't come from a long line of wealth doesn't excuse you from being able to build it. Think about how this looks to everyone else of his generation. Everyone is going out partying and having their fun and there's Noah with his family, working and building this Ark for years. I bet he was the laughing stock of his time--until it started raining. Build your business, work your overtime or part-time, pack your lunch, continue to drive your older model car that's paid off. Do whatever you need to do for as long as you need to do it in order to build your finances. Those years of hard work will benefit your family as well. Get your finances to the point where it's no longer a source of frustration for your family. How different would your kid's life be if you gave them a house that was paid off? What would your grandkids be able to accomplish with their college degree and no student loans because you paid for the education in full? Noah and his family worked for years on building that ark and because of that every generation behind him was blessed.

My wife and I followed the advice of Warren Buffet and opened a **Low Cost S&P 500 Index Fund.** Please consider adding this to your own financial ark. It's an investment account that provides a small ownership position in the 500 top performing companies.

On average the market has grown around 10% per year. My wife and I are planning to contribute $2500 per year or a little over 200 per month. At that amount, combined with compound interest, we should be able to bless him with over $100,000 by the time he graduates college. Did I mention we started this account with mostly 1-dollar bills? Investing in index funds has been a major wealth-building tool for the elite among us for years. These investment accounts will allow your money to generate money through compounded interest. You have to construct your finances to the point where they can handle life's storms without sinking you and your loved ones. It took Noah and his family 100 years to build the Ark from start to finish. Keep this in mind as you are building your financial ark. It's going to take you some years if you are building from the ground up but you can do it. For a list of brokerage options and investment calculators, visit bankrate.com.

# DAY 6: ANCHOR

*"Abram was very rich in livestock, in silver, and in gold." -Genesis 13:2*

Before the Bible called Abram a rich man, he was called to be a man in motion and to change his current living conditions. God told him to get out of his country, away from his family and out of his father's house. Abram didn't even know his destination before he departed. God told him to go "to a land that I will show you"(Gen. 12:1). I ask you, what is God calling you to get away from? What needs to exit your life in order for God to move on your behalf? Even though Abram was a man in motion, he never lost his connection to God. At every resting ground on his journey he always built his altar first. This is my question to you: what is your connection to God like? We can't have a relationship with God based solely on the purpose of our bank account balance. God didn't send His Son to die on the cross to be our ATM. How would you feel about someone who's always asking you for stuff whenever you all speak?

Abram's wealth was a by-product of his obedience to God. God told Abram to leave everything he was familiar with and start on a journey where the destination was unknown, and he did it. As you are in the process of changing your personal finances and building generational wealth, you should not let that be the sole purpose of your relationship with God. God is here to save our souls not our dollars. You shouldn't place your money in the position where you are worshipping it as god. How often do you talk about your money? How often do you complain about the lack of money available to you? Changing your finances is a part of the journey with God; it's the purpose of it. You don't have to compromise your faith, your character, morals, or do anything that God won't be pleased with to build generational wealth.

Stay connected, be obedient, and be willing to walk with God even though you don't know what the destination will be. Remember your journey doesn't just affect you by yourself; it also affects the ones you love and care about the most. Abram's nephew Lot was also with him on this journey, and he was also blessed. And the two of them had so much livestock that there weren't enough resources on the land to support them both. Their blessing was running over without compromising their faith! How many great people have fallen from great positions in life because of their compromising in order to increase their cash? Money is a resource, but God is the source. Wealth was never designed to be our master, and that's why we shouldn't serve it. We need to ensure we are doing everything we can as good stewards to ensure our money is serving us. An asset that produces passive income will be a great way to get your money to serve you.

One of my main financial goals at the time of this writing is to generate enough passive income that I won't have to trade time for dollars if I choose not to do so. Passive income is money that's being generated without you physically being there. Like a landlord with his rental property, they're probably only there to collect rent or service the house. They don't have to physically be with the rental property for them to generate income; they only have to own it. A singer who has recorded music to sell only has to produce the music to sell once, and it can be sold forever. Consider the great artists who have passed away and their estates have generated millions after their deaths. What assets do you own or will own that can produce passive income? What all could you accomplish if you could spend more time on your calling instead of your job?

# DAY 7: EXPECTING

*"So Sarai said to Abram, 'See now, the Lord has restrained me from bearing children. Please, go in to my maid; perhaps I shall obtain children by her.' And Abram heeded the voice of Sarai." -Genesis 16:2*

It had been ten years, and Sarai and Abram were still waiting on God for them to conceive their first child. Waiting on God to fulfill His promise is typically faster than waiting on Him to repair the damage we've created by rushing the process. The first words Sarai said to Abram were "See now". While we can't ignore our present-day realities, we can choose not to focus on them. When we constantly feel the pressures of life we tend to look for a way of escape even if it's not the path God has for us. We live in a culture where the results are more important than the process. But God doesn't operate in this same instant gratification culture that we do. Reflect on any mighty move of God; there has always been a process involved. Abram had the process of leaving his father's house; Moses had the process of freeing his people; Joshua had the process of possessing the Land of Canaan; and even Jesus the

Christ had the process of the cross. We can't allow our desire for results to be greater than our desire for manifesting our destiny. God doesn't operate in instant gratification so I need you to know that your finances won't change overnight, with one prayer, or with sowing one seed.

When people want things instantly they do things like purchase items on credit cards without having the cash to actually buy the items. Or buy the top of line luxury model vehicles with expensive payments just for the pleasure of having the car. Or maybe they purchase homes on the good side of town with mortgages that take the majority of their available cash. Credit cards will build interest, cars can be repossessed, and homes can be foreclosed. All of these are not pretty sights to see. Sarai wanted a baby by any means necessary, and we, as Christians, shouldn't operate in this manner. Anything of significance requires time to manifest. The best meals require hours to make not minutes in the microwave. Some of the most expensive cars are made by hand and require months to build. Some of the best marriages started out as friendships that developed into more over time. And your favorite athlete's spend countless hours practicing the game they love.

Don't allow your desires to rush you and put you into a position that you are truly not able to handle. When we rush results, it typically ends up costing us more pain. How do you think Sarai felt after she saw her husband's child being carried by another woman? Sarai grew to despise Hagar even though it was Sarai's idea to begin with. It was her present day thinking that allowed that idea to come to life. Rushed results are typically short lived. Think about all the people who win the lottery only to return to the life of poverty. They didn't go through the actual process of building wealth. They got the end result of money without actually going through the process of developing the mindset of wealth only to return to more pain of losing it all. Even when our current circumstances are less than ideal; we must continue to believe in the vision more than our present-day realities. When we focus so much on what's in front of us we tend to lose focus on what's ahead of us. What we tend to focus on will always expand. Focus on what you can do today to benefit yourself while you are waiting on the promises of God to manifest.

# BLESSED BUT BROKE: WEEK 1 CHALLENGE

## CASH FLOW ASSESSMENT

Credit Score: Equifax ____ Experian ____ Transunion ____

| Income | Monthly Total |
|---|---|
| Paychecks (salary after taxes, benefits, etc.) | $ |
| Other income (after taxes) | $ |
| TOTAL MONTHLY INCOME | $ |

My Monthly Income

My Monthly Expenses

| Expenses | Monthly Total |
|---|---|
| Rent or mortgage | $ |
| Utilities (ex. Electricity and gas)(Water) | $ |
| Internet, | $ |
| Cable | $ |
| Cell Phone | $ |
| Food (groceries, meals out, etc.) | $ |
| Transportation (gas, car payments, car insurance, etc.) | $ |
| Sinking Fund | $ |
| Personal and Family (childcare, beauty care, | $ |
| Finance (credit card, student loans, etc.) | $ |
| Savings | $ |
| Other: | $ |
| TOTAL EXPENSES | $ |

Total Income (______) – Total Expenses (______) = Cash Flow (______)

# ASSETS VS. LIABILITIES

Assets: What do you own?

| Assets | Total |
|---|---|
| Cash (on hand, checking, savings, cash value of life insurance) | $ |
| Real Estate/Property (home, land, etc.) | $ |
| Certificate of Deposit (CD) | $ |
| Investments: Saving Bonds, Gold/Silver, etc. | $ |
| Stock Portfolio: | $ |
| Retirement: IRA, 401(k), pension plans, etc. | $ |
| Personal property (automobiles, jewelry, collections, etc.) | $ |
| TOTAL ASSETS | $ |

Liabilities: What do you owe?

| Liabilities | Total |
|---|---|
| Debts (medical, credit cards, store cards, etc.) | $ |
| Mortgages (home, land, etc.) | $ |
| Student Loan Balance | $ |
| Car Loan Balance | $ |
| TOTAL LIABILITIES | $ |

# DAY 8: EXIT STRATEGY

*"Then the men said to Lot, 'Have you anyone else here? Son-in-law, your sons, your daughters, and whomever you have in the city-take them out of this place!'" -Genesis 19:12*

What is the culture of the environment in which you currently live, work, or relax? What is considered normal that's not in line with God's Word or your personal goals? The culture of the environment in which we spend time will either help or hinder us from manifesting what God has for us. At work, is most of the time spent venting and complaining about how much you hate your job? I've been on a job where that's the majority of the conversation, but many times the people who do the most complaining have been there the longest. They hate the job enough to complain about it but not enough to seek other employment. What about your home? Do you currently live in the area where you desire to have your family? If not, what is your plan to change your living conditions? Do you spend your time in or around people in poverty? If you do, chances are you will begin to think just like them and begin to see nothing wrong with it.

Let's take a look at the story of Lot. He was in an environment where the practice of wickedness was an everyday part of life. Are you in an environment where the practice of poverty is an everyday part of life? There's a saying that states this: you are the sum total of your five closest friends. How do your five closest friends feel about personal finances? Are they in the mindset and process of building? Or are they currently living in the moment? Do they see anything wrong with borrowing money, having bad credit, or not achieving financial goals? Do they say words to comfort you or challenge you in the area of your finances? Are you personally holding any of your friends accountable for building generational wealth? When we look at Lot we see that he was a man of little influence. He had to beg the angels to spend the night with him, he couldn't hold off the mob from his doorsteps, and when he told his sons-in-law that they had to flee, they laughed at him. We as Christians are called to cultivate and change the environment in which we are not to become a part of it.

Lot knew of the upcoming destruction and still didn't want to leave the city. The angels literally had to force him out. Are you in an environment that's leading to your demise and are still hesitant to leave? Maybe it's not fire and brimstone that's on the way, but maybe it's a life of unfulfillment. A life in which you are constantly robbing Peter to pay Paul. A life where payment arrangements are considered normal. A life in which you are not in position to provide yourself and your family the lifestyle that you know is well deserved? If this is your current quality of life, take you and your family out of this place. Finish your degree, work overtime, start your business, get a part-time job, change your 5 closest friends, do whatever it takes to change the environment. Read and study wealth building, attend personal finance workshops, use your social media to learn more about credit. Do whatever it takes to become that person of influence for your friends and family. Be the one to change the culture of poverty in your environment, don't become part of it. Just like the angels saved Lot from Sodom, you save your loved ones from a life of financial struggle.

# DAY 9: JUST ENOUGH

*"And when she had finished giving him a drink, she said, I will draw water for your camels also, until they have finished drinking".*
*-Genesis 24:19*

What would your friends, family, or co-workers say about your work ethic? Would they say that you are the one who always goes above and beyond? Or are you that one who always does just enough? Thomas Edison was quoted as saying, "Opportunity is missed by most people because it is dressed in overalls and looks like work." We cannot allow a minimum style work ethic to block what God has in store for our lives. The thing about being on a job that you hate, you will develop a just enough style of work. It was George Carlin who said, "Most people work just hard enough not to get fired and get paid *just enough* money not to quit." Our habits are formed out of what we repeatedly do. So if we are always working just hard enough, that will become our overall work ethic and will not just be compartmentalized to the job we hate.

When we look at the scene of what's going on here in Genesis, we are seeing that Rebekah didn't have a *just enough* work ethic. During these times they didn't have the option of indoor plumbing so they had to get their water from the well. Here we see Rebekah, a woman who could have sent her servants going to the well herself. Abraham's servant said, "Please let me drink a little water from your pitcher." He didn't offer her any kind of money at all for this drink. Not only did she do just what he asked her by getting water for him, but she also went the extra mile by quenching the thirst of 10 camels. She had the initiative to do what was needed without being asked to do it. How many times in your life have you done something that's needed without being asked to do it? It was Zig Ziglar who said, "Do more than you are being paid to do, and you'll eventually be paid more for what you do." We shouldn't allow our compensation to determine how hard we work. The Bible doesn't record her complaining about the work she volunteered to do for this stranger. Her goal was simply to focus and exceed the task at hand.

After she dominated the task at hand she was then compensated with 10.5 shekels of gold. What if she would have told him, "You're not paying me enough for all of that"? How would this story have turned out? The work came before the reward. And this is how our work ethic should be. The Bible teaches us that whatever our hands find to do that we should do it with all of our might. We should not just do what we are paid to do. Sometimes our blessing is waiting for us in that extra mile, but we will never find out if we are only doing *just enough.* My challenge to you is that you will exceed any and all tasks that come before you. Dominate your entire task at hand without complaining while you are working. I'm willing to bet that you don't want a just *good enough* marriage, just *good enough* kids, or just *good enough* income. You don't want just a *good enough* church or live in a just *good enough* community. I bet you want everything that God has in store for you. Our work ethic plays a huge part in building generational wealth. Let's ensure that our work ethic is not what's blocking us for our blessings.

# DAY 10: STEWPIDITY

*"But Jacob said, 'Sell me your birthright as of this day'" -Genesis 25:31*

How much is your appetite costing you? Here we look at one of the worst negotiations to ever be recorded in the Bible. We have twin brothers who have been fighting for the birthright since they were in their mother's womb. During these times they didn't have a Last Will & Testament that would divide everything equally among all the family members. During these times the oldest child would receive a double portion of their father's inheritance. All of the wealth that Abraham was blessed with combined with the wealth his son Issac built would be passed down to the child with the birthright. A double portion of livestock, gold, and silver would have rightfully been Esau's! But, he decided to trade everything he would have inherited for a bowl of stew. Can you picture someone offering you one bowl of stew for all of your income for the next six months? What would you say to this person? Instead of six months' income, he was trading in years of wealth to feed himself for the moment?

As Christians we should never be in the business of trading precious resources for things of little value. Are you in the business of trading yours or your kid's inheritance for stew? How much money do you currently have available for your kids compared to the amount of money you spend on manicures and pedicures? How much money have you spent in drive-thru restaurants over the years compared to how much you have saved for retirement? How much money does your transportation cost you every month? How much is the note, insurance, taxes, and maintenance combined? Now, how much money are you paying towards your life insurance policy that will benefit the generation to follow? Esau had a desire that was so great in the moment that he didn't care about the future. We will never build generational wealth as long as we are always living in the moment. You need to have your money working towards building a better future for you and your family not just being enjoyed in the moment.

Making additional "principal only" payments towards debt may not be as exciting as going on a cruise for a week. Working a part-time job to save for the down payment of your new house may not be as fun as hanging out with your friends. Working overtime to increase your retirement account balance is not as fun as going shopping. But, what are your desires costing you in the long run? Your grandkids won't benefit financially from all the vacations you took, clothes you wore, or the items you bought on clearance. The money might not seem to be a lot at the moment, but just think about if you could have invested that money and gotten a return on it. Where would your family be right now financially if you could get back half of the money you spent eating out over the last few years? You must not continue to let the present moment's desire keep you struggling financially. Start to practice the art of delayed gratification: that means even if you can spend the money in the moment you, instead, use discipline and choose not to spend it. The wealth that you will have in the future is a direct result of how you handle your money today. Don't waste the money you could use to build your generational wealth for tomorrow on the low-value pleasures of today.

# DAY 11: GROW WHERE YOU SOW

*"Then Isaac sowed in the land, and reaped in the same year a hundredfold; and the Lord blessed him."*
*-Genesis 26:12*

Everything has to bow to the Word of the Lord, even a famine. Merriam-Webster defines famine as an extreme shortage or scarcity of food. Picture being a farmer and making a living off of your land but the land isn't fertile enough to grow your food. You are basically in an environment that's not producing enough for your growth and survival. This is the stage of the land right now for our good friend Isaac. One of the key benefits of our relationship with God is to be able to get a fresh word and clarity for our specific situation. God told Isaac in verse two: "Do not go down to Egypt; live in the land of which I shall tell you." How many times have you heard someone basing a bigger success off of living in a different city? They would say if only I lived in a bigger market, then I would be successful. If you are in the city that God has called you to then you are bound to grow exactly right there. My next question to you is this: how much have you been sowing?

The Bible is teaching us that Isaac sowed in that land and reaped a hundredfold return in that same year. Even though the land was in a famine Isaac was still able to sow and reap. You're going to be hard-pressed to reap a harvest from seeds that were never sown. You need the area of personal finances to grow into your life, but how much have you been sowing? Have you been paying your tithes? Have you been giving money to those who are less fortunate than you? Can God trust you with the increase? Isaac grew his way right into a prosperous lifestyle right there in the midst of a famine. Are you in the position in which God has called you and your family to be? Are you walking in obedience? Have you been sowing exactly where you are? The Bible teaches us to give and it shall be given. What have you been giving? The truth of the matter is this: sowing is an issue of the heart and not your current balances. Isaac sowed his seed right in the midst of the famine and God took care of the increase.

Isaac grew so much in prosperity that his neighbors stopped up all of the wells in the city to try to prevent his growth (Gen. 26:15). Isaac was able to cultivate the land where he was called and with what he presently had. We must do the same thing. Cultivate means to develop. Being in the right standing with God holds more weight than a recession, budget cuts, or loss of employment. God is able to grow your wealth in the midst of your haters. Isaac had an order of protection directly from the King of the land, so no one could touch him or his wife. Can you imagine what it was like for Isaac to grow his wealth amongst people who hated him but couldn't touch him? God can do the same thing for you. You can be in an area where the environment is not typically producing and grow your way out. You can currently live in or live close to the poverty line and grow your way into wealth. It was Eric Thomas that said, "Start where you are, with what you have, because what you have is plenty". Your obedience in your relationship with God will always be bigger than your current circumstances.

# DAY 12: LONELY MONEY

*"These daughters are my daughter, and these children are my children, and this flock is my flock; all that you see is mine..."*
*-Genesis 31:43*

It was Francis Bacon who said, "Money is a great servant but a bad master." As we highlight different aspects of the life of Laban it was clear that his possessions were the head of his life. Let's go all the way back to Genesis 24:29-31 where the Bible first introduces us to Laban. In this text, Laban was impressed by objects of wealth the servant of Isaac presented to his sister Rebekah. He admired the jewelry and the ten camels that the servant had with him. During these times only the very affluent owned camels. After seeing all of this, Laban invited the servant and his camels to his house for the night. Have you ever been involved in any type of friendship just for the sake of finances? We should be looking to build wealth so we may empower change within our families and communities not just for the sake of materialism. I'm not against having nice things; I am against only having nice things. What's the point of building wealth just to please yourself and your ego? What's the point of compromising biblical values just for the sake of money?

Laban used, lied, and cheated his own family just for the sake of building up his possessions. How many times in the headlines have we seen people arrested from stealing from their companies? Do you have any friends that will do immoral things for money? What's to stop you from being their next victim? Jacob wanted to marry Laban's younger daughter Rachel and offered to serve him for seven years for her hand in marriage. Laban agreed only to recant later on his deal when it was time to fulfill his end of it. Laban probably got Jacob drunk and waited until nightfall and then gave his daughter Leah instead. When Jacob confronted Laban, he said: "It must not be done in our country, to give the younger before the firstborn." Then Laban did what most cheaters do: he took further advantage of the situation. He offered Jacob to serve him for another seven years for his daughter Rachel. Laban used his own family as pawns in order to build his wealth, which was the true head of his life. Don't be the type of person who will misuse and abuse anyone to get money. Make sure your money has its proper place in your life as your servant.

Let's fast forward to when Jacob realizes it's time for him to return back to his own land with his family: Laban's first response was for him to stay not for the sake of keeping their family together but rather for the sake of his wealth. Laban wanted to pay Jacob whatever he wanted in order to keep him there but Jacob wanted out. Jacob wanted a payment of the worst of Laban's flock to take with him as his own. Jacob's wives, before fleeing, wanted to know about their inheritance: "Is there any portion or inheritance for us in our father's house? Are we not considered strangers by him? For he has sold us, and also completely consumed our money." Once Jacob leaves with his family and possessions, Rachel decides to steal some household idols that Laban owned. Laban decides to track them down not for a family reunion but for his possessions! There is no telling what some people will do for money when it is at the head of their lives. Do everything you can in your power to ensure that your money is serving you and not controlling you.

# DAY 13: BLOOD MONEY

*"But Esau ran to meet him, and embraced him, and fell on his neck and kissed him, and they wept" -Genesis 33:4*

How many families do you right now know that are not speaking right now because of a fight concerning money? Have you ever known the Patriarch of a family to die without a Last Will & Testament and now there's a fight over the possessions? Blood family members treat each other like opponents in the battle for their portion of inheritance. I have witnessed this first hand on many occasions, and it's never good. Money shouldn't be used to create a barrier between the ones we love. Jacob, now renamed Israel, had been away for over twenty years after deceiving his own family for the birthright then fleeing for his life is now returning home. God has called him to return home and Israel is afraid for his life because he doesn't know how his brother Esau is going to respond. Reconciliation with the ones we love should happen on this side of heaven. Do you have any people you love that you haven't spoken to because of a fight about money? How would you feel if that person died and you didn't get a chance to make up?

What Jacob did to his own family with the help of their own mother was pretty low and there is no excuse for that at all. Jacob used the sickbed of his father to seize the opportunity to con his way into the birthright. If you grew up with limited resources, chances are you will have family members come out of the blue to see what they can get from sickbed family members. I highly recommend that you create and regularly update your Last Will & Testament. This will let your voice be heard after your transition without anyone having to say, "This is what he or she would have wanted." Next I would suggest that you have something of significance you leave to your family to place them in a better position financially. Their father Isaac has amassed enough wealth to bless both of his kids and we should be striving to do the same thing. Consider getting a life insurance policy big enough not only to cover your final expenses but also to bless your family. Have you known anyone to lose a family member and then turn around and have to raise funds to cover their final expenses?

I remember working on a job and getting a free life insurance policy for around $10,000. Which is not too bad of a deal, right? Or is it? I asked the representative what was the maximum payout benefit I could receive, and she responded with $100,000.00. I asked her how much would that be and she then responded with $5.00 bi-weekly. How better off would my family be for an additional $90,000.00? We have to leave our families in the best position possible and we have to secure that position with our final wishes in our Wills. We don't want our loved ones fighting over possessions that were supposed to bless them. If you have any family members that you aren't speaking to because of a money fight, I would encourage you to reach out before twenty plus years go by or that loved one transitions. Even though Jacob did Esau wrong, Esau didn't kill him. He embraced him. We only get a few people that really care about us, so let's not lose them because of a fight about inheritance. I know firsthand the pain of regret of losing time with family because of wrongdoings. Money and possessions can be replaced, time cannot. Do your part to make it right.

# DAY 14: DREAM BIG

*"Then they said to one another, 'Look, this dreamer is coming' -Genesis 37:19*

Do you have big dreams for your life? Often, when you grow up in financial lack, you can only focus on the present moment. Prayers are limited to asking God to pay off a bill or for a few dollars to save. We are conditioned to think, believe, and pray for small things. What do you believe God will manifest in your life? What would happen if you started to dream on a larger scale? What if instead of believing God to make a rent payment, you had faith you would become a homeowner? Or instead of believing God to pay a bill you believed to become completely debt free? Do you truly believe God to make you the lender and not a borrower? Make sure your dreams are not limited to your present circumstances. We serve a God who created the Heavens and the Earth, so finances are not a challenge for our God.

Let's take a look at seventeen-year-old Joseph who worked in the field alongside his older brothers in the land of Canaan. His older brothers hated him because their father loved him the most. The Bible teaches us that when Joseph shared his dreams with them, they hated him even more. Everyone doesn't have your best interest at heart. Seventeen-year-old Joseph was working in a field but his dreams were bigger than his circumstances: he dreamed that even the sun, moon, and stars bowed down to him! Like Joseph, you may have some people that despise you. This is one of the reasons why everyone doesn't qualify to hear your dreams. Everyone doesn't have your back like you think they do. I'm sure Joseph thought that if anyone was safe to hear about his dreams, it should have been his own family. The National Science Foundation did research and concluded that eighty percent of human thoughts are negative. If we think that negatively in general, would it be that hard toward be negative to someone else? Watch the responses you get when you share your dreams with your family and friends. Do they encourage and support or belittle and despise your dreams?

Sometimes your dreams can bring out insecurities in others, and they can hate you because of what they lack. It's your duty to continue to dream big dreams, pursue them, and not live down to the limitations someone else has place on you. Just like Joseph you can be working right beside them in a field, but that doesn't mean you are destined to stay there. Joseph went to help his brothers at his Dad's request and they tried to seize the opportunity to kill him. Reuben, one of his brothers, talked them out of it in an effort to get him back to their father. Before Reuben could get him back home, his brother Judah took advantage of the opportunity and sold Joseph into slavery for twenty shekels of silver. Just like

Joseph, someone might be waiting on the right opportunity to sell you out. As you are on the road to improving your finances keep in mind that everyone isn't qualified to hear your dreams. Seventeen-year-old Joseph was working in a field but in the future Joseph would be royalty. Remember to always dream without limitations and let your dreams be bigger than your present day reality.

# BLESSED BUT BROKE: WEEK 2 CHALLENGE

## 6-Month Emergency Fund

1. Calculate the total dollar amount needed to fully fund your emergency savings account.

2. Identify the fastest and most effective way to save your amount.

3. This savings account will be a buffer when challenges arise and prevent you from going into debt.

4. Make this one of your priorities; you never know what challenge's lies ahead.

# DAY 15: PREPARATION FOR LACK OF PRECIPITATION

*"Joseph gathered very much grain, as the sand of the sea, until he stopped counting, for it was immeasurable" -Genesis 41:49*

There always seems to be big differences with the way people handle their money when they have a plan for their money. Think about the engaged couple who is saving for their wedding day; the soon-to-be homeowner who just needs a 3.5% down payment on their first home; the expecting parents with their first child on the way. The employee that's just been informed they are going to be laid off in sixty days; the employee who will need surgery and will require weeks off of work for recovery time. All of these are examples of people with plans for their money. They handle their money based on their plans not their impulses. When you have a clear and immediate goal, it forces you to be intentional with your money.

This is what is going on in the Land of Egypt. They had a plan to fulfill based on Joseph's gift to interpret dreams. Let's look further into what was about to take place. Pharaoh, the leader of all of Egypt, needed something that no one else could provide for him except Joseph. The very first thing Joseph did before he met with Pharaoh was shave and change his clothes (Gen. 41:14). Even though he was fresh out of the dungeon, he didn't present himself as such. Even though you might be struggling financially right now you don't have to present yourself as such. The words you speak, the clothes you wear, the actions you take don't have to present financial struggle.

When Joseph starts talking with Pharaoh, he never mentions how his family did him wrong, how he was falsely accused of rape, or about how hard the last thirteen years of his life had been. Some people will continue to miss divine opportunities for advancement because they are always playing the victim card. Most people have a sob story; some make the choice not to dwell in it. Joseph interprets Pharaoh's dream and lets him know that there is a famine on the way and tells Pharaoh he needs to prepare for it now (Gen. 41:30). Egypt started planning for hard times in the time of abundance. This is the same principle we need to apply in our personal finances as well. I've had so many people tell me that they are comfortable with spending all of their money because they know that next paycheck is coming. What happens when the paychecks stop? What happens when an emergency arises that your current paycheck can't cover? Seventy-eight percent- of Americans are living paycheck to paycheck. It's hard to build generational wealth when you spend your entire paycheck. Like Joseph, you need to plan your way to a better future.

Joseph's plan was to save twenty percent over the next seven years to prepare for the famine. Joseph's savings plan would take years of consistency to fulfill. Building a fully funded 6-month emergency fund may take you some years but you can build it one dollar at a time. Due to Egypt's plan, they weren't wasteful with their resources during the seven years of abundance. Let's follow their example. When you have extra money, choose not to be wasteful with your resources. Consider the yearly tax return some people receive. How long does it take for some people to waste it with vacations, new cars, furniture sets, clothes, or shoes? As Christians, if we don't exercise discipline with the little extra money we receive, how can God trust us in abundance? When you take the money you have and use it for pleasure over empowerment, you secure your financial struggle. Prepare for hard times in advance so you can be fruitful in the time of affliction.

# DAY 16: OPINIONS

*"And the men are Shepards, for their occupation has been to feed livestock; and they have brought their flocks, their herds, and all that they have." -Genesis 46:32*

Your ability to build generational wealth isn't just tied to what you do full time for a living. You don't have to come from wealth to acquire, build, and leave for the next generation. Look at the lives of Abraham, Isaac, and Jacob: they were all Shepards and they built generational wealth. Egyptians looked down on Shepards. In fact the Bible tells us that shepherds were an abomination to the Egyptians (Gen. 46:34). Working for generation's day in and day out tending to the needs of their animals wasn't easy work. But, when it came time for Joseph's family to go before Pharaoh, he basically told them to own it (Gen. 46:34). It's only when you acknowledge your position in life that you're able to change it. Because of the favor upon Joseph's life, they were able to possess the best land in all of Egypt (Gen. 47:6). God's favor and their work ethic were bigger factors than their job titles. And the same holds true for us as well. Joseph's title was a slave, next prisoner, and then Governor. God is more concerned about our faithfulness to him than the title we hold on a job. So don't subscribe to the notion that wealth is only reserved for entertainers and athletes. There are millionaires in every line of work.

I've talked with people before who have accepted that their financial struggle is normal life. God is always calling us to grow from exactly where we are planted. If you were born into poverty, it is your duty to place yourself in the best position possible to grow your way out of it. Joseph's entire family was given the best land in Egypt during the time of famine because his relationship with God was rooted in obedience. Don't look down or sell yourself short with God because of your current job title or past mistakes. You won't be able to build wealth based on the gossip of other people. The next time you receive a paycheck, look for the line that says: opinions of others. Don't place such great value on the opinions of small-minded people. In today's culture, some people are more concerned with titles than their purpose in life. The title given to you by someone else shouldn't define how you see yourself. Don't allow the opinion of someone else to guide you into insecurity.

You will not be able to build your wealth beyond the point of what you think is possible. This is why having a true source of identity is vital. Don't allow what you may see on social media to make you feel insecure about yourself. People who make it their business to look down on other people typically have low self-esteem themselves. Your God-given ability to produce results will always outweigh the opinions of small-minded people. Pharaoh didn't care about Joseph's family's occupation as much as he did about Joseph's ability to produce. While some Egyptians might have been expressing their opinions toward Joseph and his family's work history, Joseph was strategizing. Let others focus on their opinions while you focus on avoiding the famine. The more laser focused you become on achieving your goals, the less you will value what other people will have to say about you. Likes, comments, reposts, or shares on social media won't get you out of debt any faster. Focus on the things that matter most in this life, and trying to impress other people isn't one of them.

# DAY 17: FOR SALE

*"Then Joseph said, 'Give your livestock, and I will give you bread for your livestock, if the money is gone" -Genesis 47:16*

What we have going on here is a story of the "haves" and the "have nots." It was around year five of the famine in Egypt and money was getting tight. So tight that some of the citizens of Egypt wanted to sell their livestock for bread because they had no money. People in desperate financial conditions often make desperate financial decisions. During this hardship, the livestock was just the first items to be sold. It eventually leads us to the citizens offering their land and themselves up for sale. What condition(s) do you have to be in for you to offer your land and yourself for sale just for the ability to eat? This makes me think about Pawnshops, payday advances, car title loan places, and government assistance. People who are in bad situations make them worse with the decisions they make. If you improve some of the circumstances, then which one of those citizens would trade all their livestock for bread? The value we place on things tends to shift, as we get deeper into financial ruins. Everything these citizens had owned, even their very bodies was now property of the government. The Bible makes no mention of these people being handicap or not able-bodied people. They had the ability to produce for themselves but have now become dependent upon the government just for their survival.

I now want you to focus on the "haves" in this story on which we are reflecting. In this instance it's the government being run by Joseph, but in reality it could be anyone with enough resources to cover the check. Think back to the 2008 recession when there was a lot of financial ruin all across the world. Not every person suffered during those hard times. High-ticket items like cars and houses were selling for much cheaper prices during that time frame. So, if you had the resources to buy them, you would have gotten a much better deal than when the economy was doing better. Joseph had worked and saved so much that he was able to take advantage of every opportunity to buy ownership of the citizen's livestock, land, and bodies. And Joseph used that form of ownership to create passive income for Pharaoh. This is a formula that we as Christians should be using: create a plan for our money, take the necessary timeframe to build up our money, use that money to create ownership in assets, and have those assets generate money for you. The Bible teaches us that twenty percent of everything they produced was to be given to Pharaoh when it was time for harvest (Gen47:24).

In life you will get to make your choices as to what side your finances will be on, the "haves" or the "have nots". God gave

Joseph the directions, but Joseph still needed to follow through on what God told him. God didn't come down from heaven and collect all the resources for Egypt to survive on. Remember, from the beginning of time God gave us the option of freewill and this is also true with our finances. We get to choose by the decisions we make or don't make with our money to live a life of financial desperation or financial abundance. Also consider that this was in year five of a seven-year famine. What could the people of Egypt have done with their resources to make it an additional two years and retained ownership? Don't let a 2-year gap be the reason you sell everything you own including yourself to another person. Be the one to buy rather than sell at a discount.

# DAY 18: WHO ME?

*"Then Moses said to the Lord, 'Oh my Lord, I am not eloquent, neither before nor since You have spoken to Your servant; but I am slow of speech and slow of tongue.'" -Exodus 4:10*

It's going to be a longer and harder journey to build your generational wealth when you are walking in insecurities versus confidence. Moses was born in Egypt during a time when there was a mandate to kill all of the Hebrew, male babies. He was born with the odds already stacked against him, but God covered Moses from birth. Moses's mother hid him for three months; however, when she could no longer hide him she took an ark and placed him in the river. Moses ends up floating right in the hands of Pharaoh's daughter who then calls for a Hebrew woman to nurse the child. And the Hebrew woman that was called to nurse this baby was Moses's very own mother. Instead of facing a life of slavery, he was now living as royalty as Pharaoh's grandchild. Who else but God could construct a life like this one? God saw fit that he didn't learn the life of slavery but that of leadership. Moses sees the burdens of his fellow Hebrews and takes it out on a slave master (Ex. 2:11). Moses saw this slave master beating a

Hebrew and ended up murdering him and hiding him in the sand. Pharaoh gets wind of this and Moses ends up fleeing Egypt to spare his own life (Ex. 2:15).

Moses ends up in the land of Midian where he lives his life as a shepherd. From living in a palace as royalty to living in the field as a Shepard may seem like a step backwards, but it was all a part of God's plan. God then appears to Moses in a burning bush to lead His people out of slavery from Egypt (Ex. 3:3). Just like Moses, God has already done some mighty things in your life. We need to be confident in what God has already done and will do in our lives. God already spared him from death as a baby, the lifestyle of slavery, and an execution for a murder He committed. And now Moses responds to God, who is talking from a burning bush, about how he is slow of speech and tongue? God wants to use you to lead your own family out of a lifestyle of poverty and I need you to walk in confidence not insecurities. Use those insecurities to keep you humble not to keep you in place. Your bank account balance will never rise beyond the amount you think is possible. You cannot let your personal insecurities hold more weight than what God has done in your life. Think about all the people that will be blessed when you can hit that next level financially.

Just like God heard the cries of His people in slavery, God is hearing your personal and your family cries in poverty. God needs a leader for your family to walk in confidence. God has already done mighty works in your life, be confident that he can change your finances. Maybe you want to know everything to do before you believe, but faith doesn't work that way. God told Moses to go before he taught Moses what he would say (Ex. 4:12). You have to start on your journey of generational wealth even though you don't know the entire process. God wants to see our confidence and faith in motion not our insecurity and fear. Focus of how you want your land of milk and honey to look and start heading in that direction. God already knows the journey and the destination, and all He needs is a faithful shepherd. There will never be perfect timing or circumstances to obtain greatness, but you serve a God who is perfect. Focus on your very next step without having to know the turn-by-turn directions.

# DAY 19: HARDSHIP FIRST

*"And the Lord said to Moses, 'When you go back to Egypt, see that you do all those wonders before Pharaoh which I have put in your hand. But I will harden his heart, so that he will not let the people go.'"*
*-Exodus 4:21*

When God sent Moses and Aaron back to Egypt to free His people, God told Moses that his heart would be hardened. All great things that we will achieve in our lifetime will require a process and our personal participation. Moses had to actually go back to Egypt and do what God had called him to do in order to free his people. Don't allow the fact that you are saved to be the reason you are lazy. We shouldn't pray for God to order our steps if we are not going to walk the path He has laid out for us. Also, remember that it's not uncommon for things to get worse before they start to get better when we are striving for greatness. Some people with health challenges have to deal with the pain of recovering from surgery before they can be free from their sickness. Mothers have to endure morning sickness and forty weeks of pregnancy before they can hold their child. And we as Christians have to sometimes hit rock bottom before we will follow God wholeheartedly. And this was the very case for Moses when he returned to Egypt to free his people.

Aaron and Moses' first stop was to the Elders of Israel and they believed that their freedom was at hand (Ex. 4:29). Aaron and Moses's next stop was to Pharaoh to demand that their people be freed from their affliction (Ex. 5:1). Pharaoh responded to them by making their work harder (Ex 5:7). The officers of Israel, the very people Moses returned to free, didn't take too kindly to their workload being increased (Ex. 5:21). When Pharaoh made the workload harder, he shifted their thinking to the present-day work rather than on the freedom that was on its way. When challenges arise we must not let it distract from the freedom that's at hand. Remind yourself who God is and what all He has done for you. That's what happened to Moses when things first got hard and Pharaoh didn't let his people go (Ex. 6:2). You must keep in mind that freedom in any form is never easy. God sent ten different plagues before Pharaoh decided to let God's people go.

Another thing I want you to keep in mind on your road to generational wealth is to have your support system. Moses had God above and Aaron by his side to support him in the process of freeing their people. Have someone in your life who's not afraid to go through the hardships of life with you: someone who's going to keep you accountable to the goals and journey that you have before you. Your journey might not be freeing slaves, but maybe it's the freeing of your family from the lifestyle of poverty. Have someone there to be able to encourage you when things get hard. Set your support system to have the right things playing in your ears when you start wondering if the process is really worth it. Send each other sermons, social media video snippets, or different biblical literature that will keep your heart and head in the process. If you already have someone like this in your life, cherish them. Thank them for helping you along in your journey. In life we typically don't get a lot of people who have our best interest at heart, so make sure you do your part to make them feel appreciated. Kind words are within everyone's budget. Make sure you give your loved ones their flowers while they're living.

# DAY 20: FORGET THE STRAW

*"Go, get yourself straw where you can find it; yet none of your work will be reduced."*
*-Exodus 5:11*

Today's entry is dedicated to all of the great people currently working a form of employment that's not their dream job. I would dare to say that the reason you are so miserable in your current line of work is because you know you aren't supposed to be there. Life is too short to spend the best hours of your best years at a job that doesn't appreciate you. Like Pharaoh, there's management at jobs that share his spirit in the sense that they believe they own you. This is why some management doesn't have any problem with treating their employees like numbers instead of actual human beings. I remember having close family needing open-heart surgery in another city, and I requested the time off; the manager responded with, "Why do you need to go there, you're not the one needing surgery?" I eventually had to go to his boss to get treated like an actually human being and get approved for the time off. The culture of your job shouldn't have the culture of Egypt and make you feel like you're in bondage. But if it does, what's your next move in order to get out of your Egypt and to your Promised Land?

Pharaoh took Moses and Aaron's request for freedom as a sign that the Hebrew slaves weren't being worked hard enough. So, in response to their request, Pharaoh made their jobs harder by removing the straw used to make bricks by the Hebrew slaves (Exod. 5:7). The straw worked as a bonding agent for the sun-dried bricks. This meant that Israel, God's chosen people, had to put in additional hours before and after work hours just to make their same quota. And this is how some jobs with the spirit of Pharaoh work: they increase the workload without any additional resources to complete the job. Some employees are singlehandedly completing the task of multiple positions with no additional pay. Some employees are forced to take their jobs home with them just to ensure their workload is completed. Those are hours that should be spent making memories with family not satisfying Pharaoh. If you are working on a job with a culture of Egypt, position yourself to leave for your Promise Land. Employment that actually has your heart; this is what I mean by your Promise Land.

I haven't worked a job yet where the employees are not complaining about what's being required of them. But the majority of those same people have been working those same jobs for years with no plans of ever leaving. Israel responded to Moses, the person who's there to lead them to freedom, by getting upset and complaining about having no straw to make bricks (Exod.

5:20). If Israel knew that they were on the way out, the straw shouldn't have mattered as much. If you are on a job that you hate, stop complaining when Pharaoh makes the job harder. Instead start planning your way out of your Egypt and into your dream job: identify what line of work that you would like to go into; pay off debts to increase your cash flow; and start saving as much cash as possible for your transition. It's amazing how your level to tolerate foolishness changes once your savings account is built up. Some people remain in Egypt far too long because they don't have any financial resources to transition. When you are working in Egypt under that spirit of Pharaoh, you are always at his mercy. Don't let the livelihood of you and your family be dependent upon a job that views you as property. You are not a slave; you are a part of God's army. Fight to make it to your Promised Land.

# DAY 21: KEEP GOING

*"Is this not the word that we told you in Egypt, saying, 'Let us alone that we may serve the Egyptians? For it would have been better for us to serve the Egyptians than that we should die in the wilderness.'"*
*-Exodus 14:12*

We, as Christians, should never justify or rationalize what's keeping us in bondage. At this point in scripture we have God's chosen people on their journey to the Promised Land and Pharaoh regrets letting them leave (Ex. 14:5). We must not lose heart at the first sign of resistance toward our goals and dreams. God never referred to His chosen people as slaves, the Bible teaches us that God called them armies. They were created to be warriors, but they learned to live as slaves. God's first command was for us to be fruitful and multiply, but we learned how to live with just enough. Israel, God's chosen people, couldn't take a slave mentality and live as free people in the Promised Land and you cannot take a poverty mentality and live in abundance. Resistance will come to you as you start your journey of building generational wealth. You will lose people you thought were friends, co-workers will talk badly about you, your car will give you trouble, and something could pop up and deplete you of your savings a couple of times. But, I need you not to lose heart.

When Israel saw Pharaoh's army in pursuit of them, they let that become their focus instead of what God had already done for them. God heard their cries for freedom and sent Moses and Aaron to lead them completely out of captivity. God sent ten different plagues displaying his magnificent might, yet Pharaoh's army seemed to be too great. Picture yourself working from sun up to sun down in the blistering heat for no pay? Imagine your body being subjected as only property to benefit another family and their desires. Think about the Israelite children. What lifestyle would they be leaving for the generation to come? Although it may not be as harsh as physical slavery, poverty is a form of bondage that we should not justify living in. We must become the warriors God sees us as and defeat this type of lifestyle. Acknowledge where you are financially, prepare yourself for the road ahead; however, never accept a life lacking financial resources as your final destination.

Let's take a look at how Moses responded to the children of Israel when their thinking became fear based: "And Moses said to the people, 'Do not be afraid. Stand still, and see the salvation of the Lord, which he will accomplish for you today. For the Egyptians whom you see today, you shall see again no more forever'". No more taskmasters, no more building wealth for another person's family, and no more crying out to God for freedom from that bondage. God placed those Egyptians in a position where they could no longer rule over Israel--at the bottom of the Red Sea. I want you to get your finances in a place where your wallet isn't making your life's decisions. Your goal is to make your choices based on what you want to do, not based on what you can afford to do. Get your money to the point where you no longer need employment from companies who think they own you, or management that treats you like slaves versus the grown adult that you are. No longer let fear, doubt, justification, or the wrong thinking keep you and the ones you love in bondage.

# BLESSED BUT BROKE: WEEK 3 CHALLENGE

## Order Your Credit Report

So many people are completely unaware of their credit score(s) and what's on their credit report. For some reason, fear positions them to just ignore their credit. Credit updates every thirty days. So, this means every month you have a chance to improve your score(s). For the most accurate reports, go directly to the source. I would suggest annualcreditreport.com for your Equifax, Experian, and Transunion report(s). You will not improve your credit ratings if you don't know what's on your report and what's affecting it. For more tips on credit, order your copy of *One Paycheck At A Time*.

# DAY 22: BIG HEART, EASY TARGET

*"Both you and these people who are with you will surely wear yourselves out. For this thing is too much for you; you are not able to perform it by yourself" -Exodus 18:18*

When I was growing up as a child my grandfather used to say: "You can't be all things to all people." And this is definitely the case for Moses with the children of Israel. All of Israel is still out of captivity and on their journey to freedom in the Promised Land, and yet after all the signs and wonders that God performed for them, they still question Him. God freed them from the bondage they were enduring as slaves in Egypt. God ensured that Israel didn't leave without their wealth, and they left with articles of silver, gold, and clothing (Exod. 12:35-36). God protected them from getting captured and enslaved again by killing all of Egypt's army, including Pharaoh. God quenched Israel's thirst in the wilderness by making bitter water sweet (Exod. 15:25). God fed them throughout their journey with meat and bread from heaven to make sure no one starved (Exod. 16:8). God even gave them victory in battle over the Amalekites (Exod. 17:13). God met all of their needs yet at every sign of adversity their first response was to complain. These are the type of people that Moses was currently dealing with.

And just like Moses, you have some people in your life who are too hard to please. The kind of person you could give the shirt off your back and they would respond by asking if you had anything else to wear. If you are the type of person that would give your last dollar to a friend in need, I ask you to stop. Learn that the word "no" is a complete sentence. People with big hearts often make for easy targets. Moses' father-in-law Jethro came into the wilderness to spend time with him after he had heard everything that God was doing (Exod. 18:5). Jethro witnessed that when people needed judgments or counsel, they turned to Moses for help from morning to evening. He said to Moses, "Both you and these people who are with you will surely wear yourselves out. For this thing is too much for you; you are not able to perform it by yourself" (Exod. 18:18). Take heed to what Jethro told Moses: you are going to wear yourself out. Certain people in your life always turn to you when they need help. In Exodus 18:20, Jethro tells Moses, "And you shall teach them the statutes and the laws, and show them the way in which they must walk and the work they must do." Similarly, teach those individuals seeking support how to overcome adversity for themselves or lead them to someone more qualified than you to deal with their issues.

Moses didn't completely turn his back on helping Israel with their problems and I'm not suggesting that you turn your back on all issues. Moses was selective with what he dealt with concerning Israel, and that's what I suggest to you (Exod. 18:22). While you are in the process of building generational wealth, you can't be all things to all people. Some people will take everything they can from someone then move to the next person before repeating the cycle. Think about how much time you spend listening to people talk about the same problem they have been struggling with for years. What position would you be in financially if you put those same hours into building your finances. There is a difference between being a helping hand and being a crutch. Don't continue to give them money: give them job applications. Help them work their way out of their own problems. If you had a bank that was always open and would always give you free money, would you ever stop going there? Don't be the open bank for the people in your life. It's going to wear you out on your journey.

# DAY 23: AVOID THE FEES

*"If you lend money to any of My people who are poor among you, you shall not be like a moneylender to him; you shall not charge him interest." -Exodus 22:25*

The children of Israel are still on their journey of freedom to The Promised Land for three months at this point in scripture (Exod. 19:1). They have been held captive and living in bondage in Egypt for four hundred years. Moses and Aaron went to meet directly with God at Mount Sinai in order to establish His covenant amongst Israel (Exod. 19:20). God wanted to establish how they should be living as His chosen people and not with all the habits they've built over four hundred years of slavery. As you personally elevate in life, certain habits can't go with you as you grow. And this is what God was currently doing with Israel by giving them the ways in which they should govern themselves. Today we are going to focus on what God told them to do concerning if they decided to lend money to the poor. God didn't want to add any additional burden on them financially by charging interest for borrowing. But, in today's culture, charging the poor is very big business. The less money you have available to you, the more typical everyday transactions will cost you.

Let's reflect on the different ways that banks charge additional monies to those with lower available balances. There are big banks in business right now that charge a monthly maintenance fee for customers who don't get a direct deposit of $250 at one time or keep at least a $1500 minimum at all times. If the majority of Americans don't have at least $1,000 saved, what are the chances they are maintaining a $1,500 minimum balance? Consider those who use their debit cards as the primary way they decide to spend. There are some debit card transactions that take days to complete and can often lead to a false balance. If you spend money you don't have the banks will gladly cover the transaction and add on an overdraft fee. If you didn't already have the money, how are you going to pay that additional fee? And what about if you need to take out a loan: the lower your credit score, the higher the bank charges you in interest. And then there's alternative banking for those citizens who can't even get a regular bank account. This typically results when a bank account is overdrawn and charged off and placed with ChexSystems. ChexSystems is a reporting agency that banks use to ensure potential customers are in good standing with other banks.

Employers are now offering prepaid debit cards to employees who don't have a direct deposit option for their salary. These types of debit cards often charge the cardholders for every transaction on the card. They basically have to pay a fee just to spend the money they already worked to earn. Some people who don't have good enough credit to borrow from a bank often turn to payday advance businesses, car title loan places, and pawnshops--all of which I have a strong dislike for because of their lending practices. A loan from a credit union or a bank could be anywhere from five to fifteen percent interest rate for borrowing. Dealing with these types of businesses can run up to four hundred percent interest. God didn't want Israel making money off of the poor, but that's now a common practice. We only covered a few options on how billions are being made off of the poor. If you do decide to bless a needy person with cash, consider making it a gift and not a loan. Lastly, make sure you are not hurting yourself and your family by being one of the poor.

# DAY 24: WAIT A MINUTE

*"And I said to them, 'Whoever has any gold, let them break it off.' So they gave it to me, and I cast it into the fire, and this calf came out." -Exodus 32:24*

At this point in scripture, Moses and his assistant Joshua are on the top of Mount Sinai receiving instructions from the Lord about priesthood and the tabernacle. Moses and Joshua were on the mountaintop for forty days and forty nights (Exod. 24:18). Moses instructed his leadership before he left that they were to handle any difficulties that arose in his absence (Exod. 24:14). One of the biggest difficulties that arose then and still plagues people this very day is that of impatience. Because Moses didn't come back as fast as Israel would have liked, they decided that they should make their own god to worship (Exod. 32:1). Before they acted on their impulse they went to Aaron, the leader at that time, and told him what they should do. Aaron decided to take gold and create a calf made of gold for them all to worship (Exod. 32:2-4). In Egypt, it was common practice for the Egyptians to worship cows. Now, if anybody knew better than that it should have been Aaron. Aaron was with Moses since he was a shepherd and witnessed firsthand everything God had done to free His children. There's nothing good to come out of acting out of impatience. Being impatient is how so many people find themselves in debt from buying things they truly can't afford because they want to rush the process to get to the result without having to endure the process of earning it God's way.

Just because things aren't moving as quickly as we would like them to doesn't mean they are not moving. Israel didn't see Moses, but he was receiving detailed instructions directly from God for their benefit. Then Israel decided to switch to another god during the process. Often, the blessing comes in the form of waiting on the instructions from God. If they had waited they never would have wasted their gold to sin against God. This is another example of how gold was never intended to be worshiped, it was meant to serve us. As a leader of your family you must hold yourself to a higher level of thinking: Aaron wasn't thinking as a leader, he was thinking just like everyone else at the bottom of that mountain. If you are to build generational wealth, you can't think on the same level as everyone else you are surrounded by. Aaron should have stood firm on the instructions he received from Moses instead of conforming to adversity of the people and creating a false god. There will always be people suggesting what you should do but that doesn't mean you should listen. Always be mindful of who you decide to take advice from because everyone doesn't qualify to give you instructions.

Once Moses confronted Aaron, he started to backtrack and gave one of the most epic excuses ever. Aaron told Moses that the calf just came out of the fire (Exod. 32:24). The Bible teaches us that Moses saw that Israel was unrestrained: no responsibility, no leadership, no patience, and no discipline were amongst the Children of Israel (Exod. 32:25). All of these are qualities that are required to change our personal finances. Where there is often little to no discipline, there is often little to no finances. Don't change your faith just because you don't see the movement you think you should see. This incident ended up physically costing the lives of 3,000 men (Exod. 32:28). Don't allow impatience to send you to an early financial grave by putting your gold in the wrong place. Let your money construct the necessary additions in your life not corrupt your faith.

# DAY 25: BE A GIVER

*". . .and they spoke to Moses, saying, 'The people bring much more than enough for the service of the work which the Lord commanded us to do'" -Exodus 36:5*

Here we have Bezalel and Aholiab talking with Moses concerning the construction of the Tabernacle for the children of Israel. Bezalel had such a high level of talent that he was placed in charge of all crafting and construction for Israel. They are basically telling Moses that they have more than enough supplies to complete the building of the sanctuary. Consider the source of those who are giving. These are all former slaves with no home to call their own, yet they are producing so much of an offering that they are being told to stop. Let's take a look at Exodus chapter 35 and verse 5: "Take from among you an offering to the Lord, Whoever is of a willing heart, let him bring it as an offering to the Lord: gold, silver, and bronze." The children of Israel also gave fine linens, stones, incense, spices and other materials needed for their Tabernacle (Exod. 35:6). And those who were gifted in craftsmanship also gave their service for the building of the Tabernacle (Exod. 36:1). Here we see different versions of the best offerings Israel had to give while they were in the wilderness. Do you have a heart for giving?

God didn't force anyone to give, but those who gave an offering did so with a willing heart. The scripture doesn't teach us that those who had the most gave the most. The scripture is teaching us that their best was given regardless of the area or the amount. What are you currently giving to God and to others, and is it your best offerings? You are called to be blessed, but you are also called to be a blessing to others. No matter the current condition your finances are in, you can still be a blessing to someone else. As you are in the process of building generational wealth, you must also look for ways to bless other people, and it doesn't necessarily have to always be with finances. Can you bless someone with a product or service, gift or talents, or maybe even giving them your time? The biggest ability for you to give stems from what's truly in your heart and not what's in your bank account. Having the heart to give doesn't always change just because you are making more money.

If someone doesn't give ten percent of a $35,000 salary, what are the chances of someone giving at a $75,000 salary if their heart doesn't change? You must develop your hearts to be a giving heart and become intentional about blessing your church, your family, your community, and causes that's dear to your heart. And if you are already a giver, ask, "how can I give more?" You must lose the idea that when you get more money, you will become a bigger giver. You can give more right now on your current level. If God can use former slaves without a home to give more than enough, then why can't God use you in your current state to be a blessing? I challenge you to look for ways to be a blessing to others. Will you provide groceries to a single parent? Will you help drive an elderly family member to appointments? Will you help someone you know find a better paying job? Will you help your family set up a retirement account? Will you help the new parents of a newborn with chores around their house? Additionally, I'm asking you to give without the strings attached to receiving. Give from your heart having only the intention of your offering to be a blessing. Sow into fertile land until God says to you, "That's more than enough".

# DAY 26: SIXTY MONTHS

*"And in the fifth year you may eat its fruit, that it may yield to you its increase: I am the Lord your God" -Leviticus 19:25*

At this time in scripture, the Lord is speaking to Moses on what to tell the congregation of the children of Israel. They are currently in the wilderness en route to the Promised Land of Canaan. Let's take a look at Leviticus 19:23-25: "When you come into the land, and have planted all kinds of trees for food, then you shall count their fruit as uncircumcised to you. It shall not be eaten. But, in the fourth year all its fruit shall be holy, a praise to the Lord. And in the fifth year you may eat its fruit, that it may yield increase: I am the Lord your God." Moses is getting a sound principle directly from God about how to yield increase. The first thing I want you to realize is that Israel is receiving this principle before they entered into the Promised Land. This is a critical aspect you must apply to the area of your finances. You must have a plan for your money before you actually receive it. So many times people make plans for what they will do with the millions of dollars from winning the lottery rather than what they will do with their tax refund. You should always have a destination for every one of your dollars. Before we can walk in prosperity we are going to have to walk in preparation.

Merriam-Webster defines planted as "placing a seed in the ground so it can grow." We must identify where we are to plant our dollars so that they can grow. God is giving us the seed to reap an abundant harvest, but we must plant it in the right ground. You must not plant your seed in ground that you will only reap entertainment for the moment. Plant your seed into ground that will grow and bring forth more seed. In other words, place your money into places where you can generate interest or equity on your money. God wasn't delivering Israel out of Egypt so that they could rent, lease, or borrow. It was all about ownership. Just like God was telling Moses to give it five years, I am asking you to give it at least five years. Challenge yourself to practice delayed gratification for at least five years. How is it that people can commit to making a car payment for five years but won't commit to building generational wealth for five years? The car is a liability and will drop in value over time. Your money planted in the right ground will only appreciate and grow in value.

Create a five-year plan for your money before today is over with and commit to sticking with it for at least five years. If your current level of debt has you losing sleep, write out every dollar you owe and focus on paying it off over the next five-years. This will stop you from paying interest and taking money away from your family. If savings is the weakest point in your finances, give it five years of building. If you went out and got a part-time job making at least $175.00 per week after you tithe, that would come out to $42,000 in savings not including any interest. How differently would your life be if you had access to that kind of savings? If you have little to no retirement money, open and invest every dollar you possibly can into your retirement account for five years to grow your retirement account. Where would you be if you take your next five years' tax refunds and only used them to build generational wealth? Because of the microwave society we live in today, we focus on the immediate gratification instead of the delayed gratification. Plant your money in the right ground, cultivate it, and give it time to grow before you yield its increase.

# DAY 27: CRAVINGS

*"Now the mixed multitude who were among them yielded to intense craving; so the children of Israel also wept again and said: 'Who will give us meat to eat?'" -Numbers 11:4*

Moses and the children of Israel have been at Mount Sinai for around a year now. God was still giving them detailed instructions on the Law and giving them structure for organizing. That's something to keep in mind: God doesn't bless where there isn't organization and structure. God was using the wilderness to organize a group of slaves into becoming the warriors He created them to be. Don't let your complaining, cravings, and lack of consideration be the reason you delay your own destiny. The children of Israel responded to answered prayers with more complaining (Num. 11:1). As a parent, how would you feel if your kids continued to act ungrateful and continued to complain about everything? Even though we are not where we want to be financially, we need to make sure that we are not in a state of constant complaining. Being faithful and consistently complaining doesn't move God to answer our prayer request any faster. How many co-workers, family members, or friends have you had in your life that only complain and nag about everything? Did that make you want to be around them and bless them with anything?

God responded to their complaining with sending a fire and consuming some of them on the outskirts of their camp (Num 11:1). Even after God responded in anger to the complaining with fire, the children of Israel responded yet again with even more complaining! This time they wanted to quench their craving for meat. Their appetite was an open door to their downfall. That craving for meat was the reason some of them ate their way into an early grave literally (Num. 11:34). How much are your cravings costing you? How much money do you spend eating out in restaurants and drive-thrus compared to how much you are investing into your retirement? Don't allow your appetite for food to be the reason you remain in poverty. Buy Tupperware containers, plastic Ziploc bags, and lunch bags for you and the family. Start to plan your meals and snacks in advance to avoid eating out and wasting money unnecessarily. I remember God saying to me, "I'm giving you the seeds to an overflow harvest, but you keep planting them in eating out". I challenge you to research to see how much money your family has spent on eating out over the past sixty days. Spending so much money on fast food slows down our process of building generational wealth. I want you to place the money that you save on eating at home into either your savings, your retirement, or getting out of debt.

When we are struggling financially, it's easy to see the negativity in life and voice that negative energy to the ones who truly love us and have our best interest at heart. Being in a constant state of frustration, we will typically aggravate and anger those closest to us. This is what the children of Israel were doing to Moses when they wanted that meat. Israel even went so far as to remember all the meals they ate freely while they were in bondage. How would it sound to hear someone reminisce about the good times of a horrible relationship? Moses had gotten to the point where He asked God to kill him (Num. 11:15). Take an assessment of how you have been communicating with and treating the ones you love. The one closest to you already knows that you are struggling financially, and they don't need to hear about it everyday. Take the same effort that goes into complaining and start expressing gratitude. Start by physically and verbally expressing your love to the ones who love you.

# DAY 28: I SPY

*"But the men who had gone up with him said, 'We are not able to go up against the people, for they are stronger than we'"*
*-Numbers 13:31*

As it is with your personal finances and especially in life, you cannot continue to be your own biggest stumbling block. Your level of faith, prayer, and thinking will always determine your quality of life. Henry Ford stated this: "those who think they can and those who think they can't are both right." The children of Israel had finally reached the Promised Land of Canaan. God instructed Moses to send out twelve leaders to spy out the land that Israel was about to be given. My challenge for you, whatever possessions you believe God is going to give you, go spy on it! If it's a house, start attending open houses in the area in which you want to live. If it's a certain type of car, go to the dealership and check it out. If it's a certain type of vacation, start researching everything you can about it. Understand me clearly, I'm not suggesting that you spend unnecessarily and jump into more debt; I'm telling you to get exposed to the possessions you believe God will bless you with. My dream car is a Lamborghini, and I've been to several of their dealerships to spy on them. I've taken my family to houses that are currently out of our price range. Don't allow your present day financial constraints and the price tag on your items to limit your belief in your ability to obtain and take possession of them.

This was an issue for the leadership that went to spy out Canaan: their fear limited their thinking. Out of the twelve spies that went into the Promised Land, ten of them came back and gave a negative report. As a leader of your family, it is very important that you don't cast reports of negativity rooted in fear. Learn not to say such things as: "we can't afford that." Instead, replace that statement with: "how can we afford that?" God is the creator of all things, even money. If God can raise the dead, how can God not help you fix your credit? Stop believing God to help you pay your rent, believe God to bless you with owning a home. Stop believing God to help you make the payment, believe God to pay the balance off in full. The studies show that eight out of ten people are living paycheck to paycheck, and the Bible is teaching us that 10 of the 12 spies didn't believe they could take possession. Don't be part of the majority of people who see struggling as a normal part of life. Have the faith that your life can be positioned in a land flowing with milk and honey.

These weren't ordinary people who went to spy on the Promised Land; these were the Leaders of the tribes! Be mindful of the leadership that you have in your life that has influence over you.

The Bible teaches us those ten different leaders (Num. 13:33) said, "we are like grasshoppers in our own sight". Insecurity cannot go with you into your land flowing with milk and honey. Place your faith in God like Caleb and Joshua, the only two spies that believed God for the possession of the Promised Land. God gave the other ten spies just what they believed, and they died right there in the wilderness (Num 14:37) in the midst of their fear and unbelief. They believed they couldn't take possession and they didn't. When they left Egypt and traveled throughout the wilderness, they continued to place too much energy into complaining and unbelief despite all God had done for them, and that eventually cost them their blessing and their life. Be a part of the minority that experiences life without living in constant financial struggle. Position yourself and your finances to experience life in a land overflowing with milk and honey.

# BLESSED BUT BROKE: WEEK 4 CHALLENGE

## Open An Online Savings Account

An online savings account is an account with a bank that's completely online.

Why an online savings account is beneficial:

- This type of account typically pays more interest on your money because the bank has fewer expenses.
- There aren't any brick and mortar locations for you to stop by, making you less likely to withdraw funds.
- This will protect you from double dipping into your savings and impulse shopping.

How to open and fund an online savings account:

- Visit bankrate.com to select an online account that best fits you. Make sure the bank is FDIC insured.
- Fund this account with direct deposit from your income to automate your savings.

# DAY 29: YOUR PLOT IN LIFE

*"And Moab was exceedingly afraid of the people because they were many, and Moab was sick with dread because of the children of Israel" -Numbers 22:3*

I know that this might come as a shock to you, but there are people who are plotting against you to ensure that you won't succeed in life. The greatness that's inside of you often speaks to the insecurities of those who don't have your best interest at heart, and this is the case with Moab and the children of Israel who are continuing their journey to the Promised Land. They had camped in the plains of Moab and struck fear into Balak, the King of the Moabites (Num. 22:1). In response to this fear Balak and his leadership sent for Balaam, a pagan prophet. Balak knew that he alone couldn't defeat Israel, so he wanted Balaam to put a curse on Israel to level the battlefield (Num. 22:11). Let's take a look at how God responded to this meeting of the minds: "And God said to Balaam, 'You shall not go with them; you shall not curse the people, for they are blessed'" (Num. 22:11). Israel was still camping in tents without their own place to call home, but God called them blessed. And you haven't made it to your own personal

Promised Land yet but God is calling you blessed. En route to your own promised land, you have to know that God is clearing the path for you. In the midst of your own wilderness experience, God will protect you for those who will come against you.

While you might be focused on your current struggles of improving your personal finances, your enemies are focused on your potential for greatness and it strikes fear into their hearts just like Balak. Their insecurities and strategies are not your concern; keep heading for your Promised Land in the face of adversity. Let's take a look at Numbers 22:7: "So the elders of Moab and the elders of Midian departed with the diviner's fee in their hand, and they came to Balaam and spoke to him the words of Balak." This king invested his time, leadership, and money to see the demise of the children of Israel based on his fear, but God wouldn't allow this plan to prosper. While you might be in or close to poverty situations, God is still your protector while you are en route to prosperity. God spoke to Balaam, the pagan prophet and told him not to go curse Israel because they are blessed (Num. 22:13). Balaam ended up going with King Balak's princes anyway, and the Angel of the Lord stood in Balaam's way (Num. 22:22). When God calls you blessed, your enemies aren't coming against you: they are coming against God.

God uses a donkey, an animal that wasn't considered to be the smartest animal to talk with Balaam instead of killing him

(Num. 22:28). The Angel of the Lord allowed him to continue his journey, but told Balaam to speak only what God tells him to say (Num. 22:35). King Balak built altars and provided burnt offerings to curse Israel, but God used that to bless his people. Balaam spoke four different prophecies and they all were used to bless Israel rather than curse them. It doesn't matter if the people who are coming against you are in leadership or not. The strategies those people decide to use will not win in the end. God often uses adversity caused by other people to push us closer to our Promised Land: bad break-ups can lead to meeting your soul mate; company downsizing can lead to the start of your own business; and you growing up in poverty should lead to ensuring your kids won't have to experience growing up with financial struggles. Use your adversity and adversaries to manifest the greatness you possess that your enemies fear the most.

# DAY 30: STRENGTHENING FROM STRUGGLE

*"And you shall remember that the Lord your God led you all the way these forty years in the wilderness, to humble you and test you, to know what was in your heart, whether you would keep His commands or not."*
*-Deuteronomy 8:2*

What if God was using your upbringing in poverty to break the generational curse of financial struggle? If you grew up in a house where finances were a source of frustration, it's your responsibility to ensure your kids and grandkids do not. You shouldn't struggle financially for years just for the sake of struggling; instead, get victory from it. Struggle should be used to develop you not to destroy you. The children of Israel were in the wilderness for forty years before they arrived to the Promised Land of Canaan. When Israel arrived in Canaan, they still had to fight to possess the land. It didn't take forty years for Israel to arrive at Canaan because of the distance—it took forty years because of their mentality.

The children of Israel who made their decisions with the slave's mindset never had the opportunity to experience freedom. The same is true for you. As long as you make decisions with the mindset of poverty, you will never experience financial overflow. It was the battles in the wilderness that God used to develop slaves into warriors. Use your struggles of financial lack to develop wealth for yourself and your family.

Building wealth as a part of your legacy needs to be a priority for you even as a Christian. Don't use your salvation by Christ Jesus as an excuse to be lazy. God doesn't send blessings overflowing with milk and honey to lazy Christians. I can't tell you how many times I've had someone tell me they are "waiting on God" with no preparation on their part. God doesn't promote us to new levels without our participation. There's no way you are waiting on God to increase your finances if you are refusing to pay your tithes. You can't possibly be waiting on God if you don't have a budget that you stick to with your money. God is not going to move on behalf of your credit score if you never pull your credit reports. How is it you are expecting God's favor to build wealth when you spend every dollar you get? God has never been in the business of wasting resources whether we are Christians or not. The thought process and the things you currently do with your money will prolong your struggle.

God heard Israel's cries and their prayers living as slaves, but they still had to go through the wilderness before they could experience freedom. The current version of yourself can't handle the blessings that God has in store for you. New clothes, new shoes, or vacations shouldn't always be the first thing that comes to mind when you receive a lump sum of money. People who don't earn or possess a lot of money mainly strategize ways to enjoy what money they do have. Start thinking about ways to build wealth at your current income level. One of the keys to reaching a new level financially is to maximize the level you are currently on. The small, consistent dollar always adds up. God didn't take Israel right out of Egypt directly into the Promised Land without the struggles of the wilderness to develop them. And God isn't going to take you from paycheck-to-paycheck to millionaire without developing your thoughts and actions into how millionaires act and think. Use the struggles of the wilderness to take you up not to take you out.

# DAY 31: DON'T FORGET

*"Then it shall be, if you by any means forget the Lord your God, and follow other gods, and serve them and worship them, I testify against you this day that you shall surely perish"*
*-Deuteronomy 8:19*

Moses is warning the children of Israel not to forget about how God brought them out of bondage and into the Promised Land. Moses is warning them not to forget to follow God's commandments, judgments, and His statutes (Deut. 8:11). Moses is presenting the choice of life with God's structure or death without it. God wants to ensure that after every material need has been met that they continue to keep His same commandments that got them into the Promised Land. Some people will allow their struggles in life to determine their relationship with God. The harder they're struggling the more time they spend with God, and the easier their challenges in life, the less time they spend with God. Moses is warning Israel before they enter into the Promised Land to not let this be their fate. Moses is also warning Israel to not to get cocky or arrogant and think they gained and created their own wealth (Deut. 8:17). God wants the same desire and thirst Israel possessed in Egypt and the wilderness to cross over with them into the Promised Land of Canaan.

I learned that the greatest amongst us in any area of life all have a great level of what I like to call achievement amnesia. This is where people continue to focus on and improve upon the actions and processes of achievement and not dwell long on a particular result. Tom Brady was once asked what was His favorite Super Bowl ring, and he responded, "the next one!" Although he had won multiple championships already, Tom wasn't dwelling on that. Kobe Byrant once told Jay Williams, "I wanted you to know that it doesn't matter how hard you work, that I'm willing to work harder than you." And Kobe had won multiple championships but still wasn't dwelling on the fact that he already had multiple rings. Denzel Washington has won multiple awards spanning over the past few decades and still has an acting coach. The greatest people amongst us will never allow one particular desired result to quench their thirst for achievement, and we as Christians shouldn't allow our blessings to cause us to lose our thirst for God.

Take heed to what Moses is telling Israel and apply it in your own life. Don't allow your arrival in your own Promised Land to cause you to grow lazy in your faith. Don't allow the fact that you have a few dollars in savings cause you to stop paying your tithes. Moses is telling Israel that they will surely perish if they stop living by the Lord's commandments. There's a saying: "Never forget the bridge that brought you over." And, in this case, Moses is telling Israel, "never forget your God who brought you out of Egypt, through the wilderness, and into the Promised Land." People who are completely satisfied with only a taste of victory won't have its taste very long. Once your finances start to change for the better, continue to build and improve upon them: don't start to spend recklessly just because you have been approved for credit cards with higher limits; continue to budget each individual dollar as if it was your last; and don't add any additional debts for you to pay off. Practice achievement amnesia and continue to improve the actions and processes that caused your finances to change for the better. Refuse to let the fact that all your bills are current cause you to lose the hunger to improve your finances. Place yourself in a position to be able to bless your grandkids and beyond. Remember the goal is to build wealth that can be passed through generations.

# DAY 32: CHOOSE LIFE

*"I call heaven and Earth as witnesses today against you, that I have set before you life and death, blessings and cursing; therefore choose life, that both you and your descendants may live." -Deuteronomy 30:19*

At this point, Moses is preparing Israel for his death and the transition of Leadership to Joshua. Moses is reiterating to Israel to make the right choices for themselves and their descendants to come so that they may live. The choices we make and the amount of discipline we exercise will always have an effect on the generations to follow. The first generation of Israel to leave Egypt made enough bad choices that they never had the opportunity to step foot on or even see the Promised Land of their forefathers Abraham, Isaac, and Jacob, and the following generation would make enough bad choices to lose the Promised Land that they inherited. Free Will has been available to us ever since the Garden of Eden. God is a true gentleman and He would never force us to do anything—He always gives us a choice. You must realize that discipline and decision-making can be an inherited trait. The seeds you are planting with your actions today will be the fruit your descendants reap tomorrow.

Make the right choices today in order to ensure that you are leaving assets behind for the next generations to build upon. By now, you should already have a completed Last Will and Testament. Remember that nothing breaks up a family like the fight over a loved one's assets. Strive to reach for assets that include at least one home that's completely debt free. Additional small, principal-only payments to your mortgage balance can save you thousands of dollars in interest over the lifetime of a mortgage. Another asset you can choose is a sizable life insurance policy. You can aim for a minimum of six figures and as much as your budget will allow. The best assets are those that generate passive income. Passive income is income that you don't have to trade your physical time in order to receive the income. Some examples of assets that produce passive income are: original books you write, musical albums you create, rental properties you own, and dividends from your stock portfolio. Make financial choices today that will create generational wealth.

What are you currently teaching your descendants about personal finances? In this Information Age, you have the option to learn as much as you want on any subject. Make the choice to schedule time regularly to educate yourself and your family in the area of finances. Also, let your kids and/or grandkids see you executing the things you learn. Let them see you choosing discipline as it relates to your money. Let them see you creating and sticking to your budget. Let them see you reading and studying different investment opportunities. Discipline is always a personal choice because of freewill. I believe your kids and grandkids will choose to exercise discipline if that's the culture of the household in which they were raised. Israel had the favor of God upon their lives, but they still had the heart and mind of making bad decisions. Israel's choices would eventually cause them to lose the Promised Land and the favor of God. Reduce the risk of your descendants losing the wealth you will build over the years to come by teaching them to exercise making better choices. Ensure you have an inheritance to leave behind and teach your family how to build upon what you are leaving before you transition.

# DAY 33: INSTRUCTIONS

*"And the seventh time it happened, when the priest blew the trumpets, that Joshua said to the people: 'Shout, for the Lord has given you the city!'" - Joshua 6:16*

Moses, the servant of the Lord for the children of Israel is now dead and leadership has transitioned to his assistant Joshua the son of Nun (Josh. 1). After the death of Moses, Joshua received instructions on how to take possession of the Promised Land. Joshua's first order from God was to lead Israel to cross the Jordan River similar to how Moses and the first generation of Israel had to cross the Red Sea. Joshua commanded his officers to (Josh 1:11) tell the children of Israel to get prepared before they were to cross the Jordan. Joshua sent (Josh 2:1) 2 men to spy out the Land, especially Jericho, and the Bible teaches us that Jericho was securely (Josh 6:1) shut up because of Israel. That means that Jericho was already prepared to defend their land against the children of Israel: the two men went to the Rahab the Harlot's house, which was located right along the city wall. When the King of Jericho heard of this, He wanted Rahab to give the men up. But Rahab lied about their location to protect them and her loved ones (Josh. 2:5). Rahab knew that their land was about to be under new ownership and wanted her act of kindness to spare her life and the lives of her family (Josh. 2:9, 12).

In the natural, Jericho seemed to be in a better position to win the battle but Israel had the favor of God with them. And the favor of God will outperform any defense system(s) that mankind can think up. This is why Jericho's hearts were melted and there was no courage left among them. After Israel crossed the Jordan and was circumcised, Joshua received instructions on how the destruction of Jericho would take place. Joshua stayed in a constant place of receiving instructions and preparation, and this is how we, as Christians, should handle our finances. Shouting just in itself will not move God to change our finances. You can scream as loud as you want and tear up every aisle in the church, but your money will never change if you never take the time to receive instructions on how to become a better manager of your finances. As your finances grow, you should always be thinking in a state of preparation of what's next. Before you can manifest, you must prepare; and before you can prepare, you must receive instructions on how to prepare. You can't just jump right to the manifestation stage.

Remember, Israel had been on a forty-year journey before they had the opportunity to take possession of the Promised Land. It's never a question of if the blessing is available: it's a question of can we handle the blessing. Do you have the discipline and consistency to properly handle what it is that you are praying and believing God for? If God gave you all the money your heart desired, would you pay your tithes? If you had the millions, how many other people would you be a blessing to? At every stage of Israel's journey, they had to receive instructions, and they had to execute what they were told. Lives were lost when they didn't act on what they were told to do. What has God instructed you to do in the area of finances that you haven't completed yet? What are you currently preparing your finances for? You prepare your finances to stay in a season of struggle when you are not receiving instructions for growth. The manifestation of abundance doesn't come to pass without receiving instruction and exercising preparation.

# DAY 34: THE STEPPING STONE OF FAILURE

*"So the Lord said to Joshua: 'Get up! Why do you lie thus on your face?'" -Joshua 7:10*

In the book of Joshua, the children of Israel have started to take possession of the Promised Land and have just defeated Jericho. Now, they are preparing to take possession of the city of Ai. Joshua sent men to go spy out the country just as he did with Jericho. The spies returned to Joshua and suggested not to send everybody, but only a few thousand (Josh 8:3). Israel assumed that victory would be easy because Ai's numbers were few, but victory was not in store for Israel in the first battle. In fact, Ai had the warriors of Israel running away and killed thirty-six of them in the process. After the first battle, Israel lost their courage and their hearts were melted (Josh. 7:5). Joshua tore his clothes and went to the Lord in prayer (Josh. 7:6). The very first words the Lord spoke to Joshua were: "Get up!"

How many times have you allowed failure to lead you to a low place in your life? Low places like insecurity, loneliness, or even depression to name a few. If you are not in a healthy place mentally because of an experience with failures in any area of life, it's time to get up! Failure is a system that doesn't work. It is not your identity. When you experience a failure in your life, don't ignore or run from it. Identify what it was in that system that didn't work and what needs to be different the next time.

God told Joshua exactly what it was that led to this defeat: Achan, the son of Zerah had taken things from Jericho that the Lord told Israel to abstain from taking (Josh. 7:1). Because of his decision, Achan had broken the system that was working for Israel and drove the Lord to anger. Let's take a look at what Achan had to say in verse twenty-one when He was face to face with Joshua: "When I saw among the spoils a beautiful Babylonian garment, two hundred shekels of silver, and a wedge of gold weighing fifty shekels, I coveted them and took them." Achan let greed get the better of him and traded in the favor of God for silver, gold, and a robe. As a result, Achan and his family were stoned. Have you ever experienced failure due to someone else's decision? Even so, it's still your responsibility to get up and correct the situation.

After Joshua identified and fixed the part of the system that was broken, God told him not to be afraid or dismayed and to go back to Ai (Josh. 8:1). The experience of failing can often crush your heart in pursuit of success. Just like God told Joshua, do not be afraid or dismayed. Although you might personally feel like a failure in certain areas, remember it's not you: it's something within the system you are using that isn't working properly. What is it in the area of your life that's broken? Is it your finances, relationships, career, health? Identify exactly what has led to lack in these areas. What are you going to do to fix these issues? Joshua didn't just stop at prayer. He executed the instructions from God. Joshua didn't let a temporary defeat at the city of Ai stop him from possessing all of Canaan. Israel defeated and took possession of the land of Ai using a specific strategy from God. It can be challenging to hear from God when you are at a low point in your life. Get up! Create a new system and use your old failures as building blocks on your pathway to success.

# DAY 35: DECISIONS

*"So the people answered and said: "Far be it from us that we should forsake the Lord to serve other gods" -Joshua 24:16*

Joshua was giving His farewell address and warning to the leaders of Israel before His passing. Joshua, at this time, was believed to be around eighty years old and decades had passed since He led Israel across the Jordan River. In this passage, Joshua is warning the leaders of Israel before the entire congregation not to cling to remnants of the nations that were still among them (Josh 23:12). Joshua knew association and fellowship with those who worshipped idols would lead Israel away from the one true God. The difference-maker for Israel has always been the favor of God upon their lives, but if the children of Israel turned from following the one true God, Israel would perish from the land that God has given them (Josh. 23:13). There was no outside obstacle from the exodus of Egypt to taking possession of Canaan that could have stopped Israel. The greatest enemy of this time and even in your own personal life has always been within. Your current personal finances are a direct reflection of the decisions you chose to or not to make.

There are outside forces that are designed to separate you from your money but ultimately you have the final say so on your financial well-being. Your employer paying you a wage that's lower than what you feel like you're worth could be outside of your control, but who's forcing you to stay at that job? Your bills might be higher than what you would like to pay, but who is responsible for creating them? It's the decisions that we choose to make that often times lead us away from the favor of God in our lives. Outside of the favor of God is the most dangerous place to live. That wasn't the favor of God that blessed you with the financing to get that car at a 20% interest rate. It wasn't God who told you to get every dollar for your mortgage that you qualified to receive. It was your decision making that led you to make those financial moves. Joshua was telling Israel that their decision-making would either produce God's favor or His absence in their lives. The same holds true for our personal finances: the results will be based upon our decision-making. It's going to be impossible to build generational wealth as long as you lose the battle to the enemy within. You lose to the enemy within [yourself] when you take actions that you know don't align with your current or future financial progress.

With this farewell address, Joshua wanted to ensure that Israel had their personal relationship with God, and He also addressed the leadership first. As a leader of your family, you will help mold the direction of your family. You must keep this in mind: the type of leadership will determine the type of legacy. And as a leader, you shape the environment. Joshua warned them of the downfall that would come from the wrong types of associations with those within their environment (Josh. 23:12). Everything they worked and went to war for would be lost. Never have those in your environment who will lead you to your demise. Just like Joshua, make sure the ones you love and care for are set up for success without you having to be there. Some forms of dependency can be not only unhealthy in life but also very dangerous especially as it relates to your personal finances. Teach your family how to generate money on their own without having to borrow. Teach your family to achieve multiple streams of income. Teach your family this African proverb: "When there's no enemy within, the enemy outside can do us no harm".


121

# BLESSED BUT BROKE: WEEK 5 CHALLENGE

## Create an additional stream of income for 90 Days

Select your route to generating a new consistent stream of income: starting your business, a new part-time job, overtime at your current job, or freelance work. Do whatever works best for you to improve your current financial situation. Use this new income to empower yourself to build wealth rather than to enjoy. Too many people make room to enjoy their money before they should, and that's why they're still broke! Don't let this be you.

# DAY 36: YOUR BELIEF

*"And the Angel of the Lord appeared to him, and said to him, 'The Lord is with you, you mighty man of valor!'" -Judges 6:12*

Here we have this generation of Israel that was doing evil in the sight of the Lord, so God delivered them into the hands of the Midianites for seven years. That's right—God's chosen people had been delivered into the hands of their oppressors (Judg. 6:1). The inheritance that had taken hundreds of years and multiple generations to achieve had been lost because of the lack of leadership and follow-through. The children of Israel had forsaken the God who had delivered them out of Egypt and started to worship the pagan god Baal (Judg. 2:13). Instead of Israel shifting the culture away from the remnants of Canaan, they became part of it. Achievement should never be based on merely acquiring something for a limited time; rather, it should be measured on maintaining your accomplishment for generations. Israel had broken their relationship with God, so their reality was broken. Instead of Israel enjoying the land overflowing with milk and honey, they were living inside of caves in the mountains (Judg.

6:2). Meanwhile, God chose to use Gideon to save Israel from the hand of the Midianites.

When the Angel of the Lord appeared to Gideon, God called him A Mighty Man of Valor. Merriam-Webster defines valor as "great courage in the face of danger, especially in battle." This isn't exactly how you would describe someone who's currently hiding in a pit to avoid being attacked. The next thing God told Gideon to do was to save Israel (Judg. 6:14). Gideon responded: "O my Lord, how can I save Israel? Indeed my clan is the weakest in Manasseh, and I am the least in my father's house." Gideon sees himself, and is trying to convince God that He's chosen the wrong person. There's a saying that applies here: "Whenever we fight for our limitations we get to keep them." Gideon has an internal perception of being weak based on his broken reality that's based on a broken relationship with God. When Gideon saw himself as weak, he shaped his reality around the identity of being weak. Your reality will oftentimes be rooted in your internal perception of yourself. The same holds true with your finances.

As long as you internally identify as someone in poverty, your reality will always be rooted in poverty. Your financial situation will always be based on the story you tell yourself about money. The majority of people who struggle financially learned their financial decision making from other people who struggle financially. They tell themselves things like, "you can't take it with you," "you only live once," or "you work hard, enjoy your money." If you believe you will always have a car payment, you will. If you believe you can't afford to buy a house, you won't. If you believe you don't make enough to save, you will never build your savings. If you believe the only way to generate wealth is through backbreaking labor, you will work until you die. Once Gideon internally perceived himself differently, he was able to start the process to change his external reality, and you have to do the same thing. Gideon received instruction from God, who was not of his current culture. When it comes to money, start listening to those who are not of your culture and have achieved the financial status you desire. Don't build your financial reality from a culture that's built on false information. When it comes to your generational wealth, your internal perception will become your external reality.

# DAY 37: LEADERSHIP

*"So they gave him seventy shekels of silver from the temple of Baal-Berith, with which Abimelech hired worthless and reckless men; and they followed him" -Judges 9:4*

Many great movements will rise or fall based on the quality of their leadership. And when the leadership is more focused on themselves rather than their mission, the mission cannot be achieved. Before Gideon's death, the men of Israel wanted Gideon and His family to become ruler over Israel (Judg. 8:22). Gideon responded with his mouth to their request by saying "the Lord shall rule over you"; however, but by Gideon's actions, he said 'yes, I will receive your worship. Gideon's actions show him refusing to call the people to worship and build an altar to God for Israel's deliverance as his predecessors had done (Judg. 8:23). Gideon also collected forty pounds of gold to create an idol (Judg. 8:22-27). What's inside of someone's heart, especially leaders, will eventually be exposed regardless of what their words tell you. God didn't call Gideon to become ruler of Israel; God called him to save Israel from oppression. The best leaders lead from a place of servanthood not pride, and that spirit of pride would come full force in

Abimelech, one of Gideon's sons. Abimelech, which means "my father the king," was the son of a Canaanite woman. The very people that God warned Israel that would lead to their demise, was the mother of one of Gideon's seventy sons (Josh. 23:13).

Abimelech conspired amongst His mother's family to become ruler of Shechem because of his own self-interest, not to add value to the people. His mother's family agreed to Him becoming king and paid him seventy shekels of silver. With the silver, he hired what the Bible called "worthless and reckless men" (Judg. 9:4). Leadership that's rooted in self-interest will use resources and people to further their own interests. I want you to consider the management under which you might work. Are their leadership traits based on the growth of your company as a whole or based solely on their individual stats? How is it possible that companies can pay out bonuses to leadership and have layoffs at the same time? Or maybe it's not about the money for you; maybe it's solely about how they treat you as an individual. Does your company/manager view you as a position filled or a person? As I mentioned earlier, I personally remember asking my manager at that time I needed the day off because my sister was having heart surgery out of town. He responded, "Why do you need the day off, you're not having surgery?" Years later, I remember another instance where I requested the day off in advance to accompany my wife to the doctor. Management told me I couldn't go with my Wife to the doctor because they already had two other people off. On both occasions, I put my family before the job.

Abimelech killed sixty-nine of his seventy brothers to secure his position as the only King. People who will do anything to get into leadership, especially immoral things, are not the leaders you want to follow. This isn't the kind of leadership you need to be under which you are attempting to build your generational wealth. Abimelech's leadership would eventually lead to the destruction and deaths of many people. Although it might not be a physical death you might be facing, working for the wrong leadership can and will kill the seeds of greatness that's inside of you. Abimelech sowed salt into the grounds of Shechem to make it infertile for 150 years (Judg. 9:45). Today's management might choose low wages, unpaid benefits, or missed promotional opportunities instead of salt to stop your progress.

# DAY 38: HURT PEOPLE, HURT PEOPLE

*"And it came to pass, when he saw her, that he tore his clothes, and said, 'Alas, my daughter! You have brought me very low! You are among those who trouble me! For I have given my word to the Lord, and I cannot go back on it.'" -Judges 11:35*

The Bible teaches us that Jephthah the Gileadite was a mighty man of valor (Judg. 11:1). The Bible also teaches us that Jephthah was the son of a harlot. Jephthah would grow up and would eventually be rejected and cast out by his own brothers because they didn't share the same mother (Judg 11:2). The pain felt from that rejection cut Jephthah to his core based on how the Bible teaches us he responded. Jephthah responded by banding with worthless men and going out raiding together (Judg. 11:3). Why else would a mighty man of valor band with lowlifes and commit crime together if He wasn't living based on the pain he was feeling? Making emotional decisions rooted in pain will only lead us further away from the healing we desperately need. As Christians, we should never make decisions based on the emotions we feel at a given moment, and we should not build our lives around the pain we felt at any given time. It's very common for the very people who rejected you and caused you so much pain to be the very ones who need you in their lives. This was the case with Jephthah: years later the elders of Gilead needed him to lead them in war against the people of Ammon (Judg. 11:4). Once rejected by the people of Gilead and now Commander of Gilead, Jephthah went to war with the people of Ammon.

The Bible teaches us that the Spirit of the Lord came upon Jephthah before he entered into battle, but in the very next verse, Jephthah willingly makes a vow to the Lord to sacrifice whatever comes out of his front door when he returns home in peace as a burned offering (Judg 11:29, 31). Jephthah, like many people, made a commitment from an emotional place. Oftentimes when you are emotional, you can't make sound logical decisions. Emotions such as fear should never lead your decision-making, and you should definitely not use these times to make a commitment. Jephthah allowed his emotions to end the potential of his only child's future (Judg 11:34). Your emotional decision-making doesn't only affect you, but it also affects the ones you hold dearest in your heart. Are you currently allowing your emotions to ruin the future with the ones you love? Have you ever said or done anything out of anger that ended a relationship with a loved one?

Have you allowed your rejection issues from your past to keep you from experiencing love because of the fear that you might get hurt? Have you ever committed to a relationship based solely on the pleasure it made you feel even though logically it wasn't the right choice?

Pleasure, fear, anger, and happiness are emotions that shouldn't be at the forefront of your spending habits. It's going to be hard for you to build wealth when your emotions are guiding choices. Your emotions can also lead you to not holding yourself accountable. Once Jephthah returned home and His daughter came to greet Him, Jephthah blamed her for bringing trouble on him. Jephthah was the one who willingly offered his daughter as a burned offering to the Lord. You are the only one responsible for your emotions and the actions you make based off of your emotions. Generational wealth, your relationships, and/or your careers should never be based on how you feel at a given moment. Hold yourself accountable to allow your emotions, thoughts, and actions to be rooted in the Word of God not emotionalism.

# DAY 39: WEAKNESS FOR SALE

*"When Delilah saw that he had told her all his heart, she sent and called for the lords of the Philistines, saying, 'Come up once more, for he told me all his heart. So the Lords of the Philistines came up to her and brought the money in her hand.'" -Judges 16:18*

The children of Israel had reached their lowest point on their way to hitting rock bottom. Israel was in the midst of captivity, and God sent Samson to deliver Israel from the Philistines. Samson was the last judge of the children of Israel and the strongest physically. As much strength as Samson possessed, he wasn't strong enough to control his intimate desires. Don't allow what's behind your zipper to lead to your demise. The Bible teaches us that Samson saw a woman in Timnah that he found beautiful and wanted her as his wife (Judg. 14:2). What is easy on the eyes can sometimes be hard on your life. Making the decision to be intimate with someone because of their appearance who you aren't supposed to be with whom can be fatal. The Philistines knew that Samson couldn't be defeated by strength alone, so they used his area of weakness to defeat him. No matter how strong you are in a given area, your true test of strength comes from how you handle your weaknesses. It's like the saying, "a chain is only as strong as its weakest link."

After being intimate with multiple Philistine women, Samson loved a woman named Delilah. The lords of the Philistines offered Delilah a bribe to identify the true source of his strength (Judg. 16:5). The amount of the bribe was 1,100 pieces of silver from each of the five lords, and that amounted to 550 times her yearly salary. The Philistines were able to purchase Samson's downfall through his weakness of being intimate with the wrong people. Some things should never be up for sale, especially your purpose. How many present-day relationships are destroyed because of physical and/or emotional intimacy with the wrong person? If you are not careful, you can allow what's behind your zipper to lead you to a place that your wallet can't get you out of. There are fortunes that are lost between the sheets: don't let this be your story. And it's not just about money: it can be lost relationships with kids, friends, and other family members. Your character and reputation can be damaged beyond repair. Never be in a position to place your pleasure over your purpose.

Samson decided to stick around, even after multiple unsuccessful attempts from Delilah to have him killed. She then decided to weaponize Samson's love for her in order to make him completely vulnerable. Many people use an unhealthy version of love as a Trojan horse to fulfill their individual desires. Samson killed hundreds of Philistine men in battle but lost to the Philistine woman Delilah in bed. After the Philistines were finally able to subdue Samson, the first thing they took was his eyesight. Don't forsake your ability to fulfill the vision you have in your heart by what's pleasing in your sight. Just because it looks and feels good at the moment doesn't mean it's good for you in the long run. Samson, who was once known as the destroyer of their land, was reduced to public mockery (Judg. 16:25). Intimacy with the wrong person creates a debt that money alone will not be able to pay off. Intimacy is sacred and should be treated as such. Sometimes the strongest among us not only fights temptation, but they avoid it completely.

# DAY 40: PROTECT WHAT'S YOURS

*"So all the men of Israel were gathered against the city, united together as one man" -Judges 20:11*

At this point, there's still no solid communication, no real leadership, and no consistent relationship between God and this generation of the children of Israel. When mankind isn't headed in a direction towards the true and living God, down is the only direct you can go. One thing you have to understand about sin nature is that it's progressive and will always grow desire and thirst for things that are not of God if we allow it to do so. Sin nature is at the very core of why so many families are living in a broken unhealthy state. The Bible teaches us about an unhealthy relationship between a Levite man and his concubine. The concubine left the Levite man to return to her Father's house for four months (Judg. 19:2). After such time, the Levite man left the remote mountains of Ephraim to Bethlehem in Judah to win her back (Judg. 19:3). On their return trip home they found lodging with an old man in Gibeah as the sun went down (Judg. 19:15).

Once there, perverted men surrounded the old man's house and began beating on the door for the old man to bring the Levite man outside. These perverted men wanted to know the Levite man carnally.

The old man who owned the home offered these perverted men his virgin daughter and the Levite's concubine in exchange for their own safety (Judg. 19:24). The Levite man didn't defend himself or the young woman and gave these perverted men his concubine and they abused her all night long and didn't let her go until the morning time (Judg. 19:25). This young woman made it back to the doorsteps of the old man's house where she died. As the leader of your family, you should always place yourself in a position to protect the ones you love. There's no point in building generational wealth for your family if you are not willing to protect them. We are living in evil times, and I highly suggest you take all the necessary steps your state requires to obtain and carry your legal concealed weapon. Purchase and get familiar with your weapon; make trips to the shooting range on a consistent basis. Just because you are a Christian and carry your Bible doesn't mean you shouldn't carry your gun. Sign up and train your family with hand-to-hand self-defense measures. Have an alarm for your house and a plan to defend your home from intruders. Stay aware of your surroundings while you're traveling and in public places. These suggestions aren't to place you in a state of paranoia but rather a mindset of protection.

The Levite man returned home and informed His fellow children of Israel of what took place in Gibeah. Israel united and arose as one man for justice against the perverted men in Gibeah (Judg. 20:11). Once the children of Israel arrived in Gibeah demanding them to deliver up the perverted men so they could put them to death, the children of Benjamin united to go to battle against the children of Israel. The Bible teaches us that Gibeah had seven hundred select men whom could all sling a stone at hair's breadth and not miss (Judg. 20:16). This teaches us that the children of Benjamin were trained and ready to do battle. Just like in Gibeah, there are people who are in this world looking to commit evil acts. Pray and fast for God's continuous protection upon you and your family. But, in addition to fasting and praying, do everything in your power to defend yourself and the ones you love. As a Christian, make sure that prayer is something that you do. Don't become prey.

# DAY 41: THROUGH THICK & THIN

*"Where you die, I will die, And there I will be buried. The Lord do so to me, and more also, If anything but death parts you and me."*
*-Ruth 1:17*

Identifying yourself as the victim in your life doesn't lead to success. So many people love to share with everyone who will listen on how they were done wrong in their lives. I would not disrespect the pain you might have been through, but you also shouldn't allow yourself to live the rest of your life from a place of pain as a victim. This is the story of Ruth. Ruth didn't allow adversity in her life to stop her from seeking to improve her circumstances. Ruth, like many of having family to depend on for support, but Ruth didn't allow that to prevent her from having a support system. Naomi, who is Ruth's mother-in-law, lost her own husband and both of her sons, and that created an entire family of widows. Naomi wanted both of her daughters-in-law to return to their mother's houses. Naomi felt that this was the best way for her daughters-in-law to find husbands again. Despite having her own grief to deal with, Naomi wanted to put the interest of others at the forefront. Naomi is teaching us that even in the midst of personal adversity, we can still add value to the lives of the ones we love.

Ruth refused to leave Naomi's side, left her hometown of Moab, and returned to the city of Bethlehem with Naomi. Once in Bethlehem, Ruth went right to work in the field of Naomi's wealthy relative named Boaz. I can't tell you how many times I've heard, "I'm just waiting on my Boaz". Ruth is teaching us that we have to be a proactive part of our own blessings. Ruth didn't play the victim card by telling Boaz how hard she had it in life. Ruth didn't ask for a loan from Boaz until she got her next check: Ruth seized the opportunity to go to work for herself and Naomi. When it comes to improving your personal finances, you're going to have to choose being proactive over playing the victim card. Your bank account doesn't grow every time you convince someone that your life is full of adversity. Ruth was in a foreign land without her parents, a husband, or any wealth and she didn't allow any of that to eliminate a strong work ethic. You shouldn't allow your Christian faith to be a justification for you to be lazy. Ruth is teaching us that even in our seasons of lack and adversity that we must choose perspiration over relaxation.

Boaz noticed Ruth as she was working, not complaining, and asked about her from one of his servants. Boaz is showing us that sometimes your character can get you an audience that your lack of resources cannot. Boaz, like many other wealthy people, helps those who choose to help themselves. Even in your season of financial lack, don't look for handouts; instead, consistently look for opportunities to improve your own and your loved ones' circumstances. While at mealtime with Boaz, the Bible teaches us that Ruth ate and kept to take some back (Ruth 2:14). Ruth didn't consume all the food she could even though it was available. Ruth had worked all day long in the field but still exercised enough discipline to save some food for Naomi. This is another good principle you should apply within your personal finances: even though you're going through hard times, you worked hard for it, and it's available to you, don't consume all of your resources just because they're available. Oftentimes your blessing is attached to being a blessing to someone else. Ruth returned with Naomi to the city of Bethlehem to add value to the life of her mother-in-law, and in the midst of doing that, she met her future husband. Even in times of struggle, make the time to add value to someone else while also exercising a strong work ethic as you wait on your own blessing.

# DAY 42: PROVOKED

*"So it was, year by year, when she went up to the house of the Lord, that she provoked her; therefore she wept and did not eat"*
*-1 Samuel 1:7*

Have you ever worked with someone whose sole intent seemed to be to make your life miserable? Maybe it was a family member or even possibly someone you serve with in church ministry? This was the situation between Hannah and Peninnah: they were both married to Elkanah. The Bible first teaches us that Peninnah had several children, but Hannah didn't have any kids. The Bible also teaches us that Elkanah loved Hannah more than he did Peninnah. Let's take a look at 1 Samuel 1:5: "But to Hannah he would give a double portion, for he loved Hannah, although the Lord had closed her womb." The Bible doesn't make mention of Elkanah loving Peninnah or giving double portions because of his love for her. Peninnah would use Hannah's barrenness to provoke her and make her life miserable (1 Sam. 1:6). I want you to place yourself in Hannah's shoes. Picture yourself being in a position that's completely outside of your control that's preventing you from achieving your heart's desire. And having someone whom you are close to rubbing the fact that you haven't reached your achievement in your face on a consistent basis. How would you respond to this particular ridicule?

At some point, you are bound to come across someone who will make it their life's mission to make your life miserable. Peninnah provoked Hannah to the point of tears and to a place that she wasn't eating (1 Sam. 1:7). Some people will find pleasure in leading you into a place of depression—don't give them that joy. Maybe your Peninnah is in management in your place of employment and their goal is to get you to quit. Or maybe they just want you to snap and lash out so you can become that person they made you out to be in their private conversations. I've been on jobs with a Peninnah, and all of those times I've realized that they were just miserable people. If you work with a Peninnah, here's my practical advice to you: write down all your grievances and take them all to leadership. You spend too much of your good hours of the day at your job for it to become a place of harassment. Stand up for yourself in a professional manner and don't allow yourself to be bullied. Hannah took all her grievances to the Lord in prayer—the source of her solution.

Use your Peninnah as fuel to reach your achievements and don't allow them to shift your mental state into a place of barrenness: a place mentally where all you are focusing on is that person who's tormenting you and stealing all of your joy. Or maybe you are your own Peninnah because of a past failure. Remember that failure is a part of a system that didn't work; however, it is not your identity. Maybe it was a relationship, a business idea, or a career move that didn't go as you planned. You can't allow that past failure to continue to speak to the vision that God has placed in your life. Don't allow past failure's to become your Peninnah and lead you into a depression. Allow your adversity and your adversaries to push you closer to God just like Peninnah did for Hannah. God blessed Hannah with a baby boy and named him Samuel, which means "Offspring of God." Samuel was later one of many kids Hannah was blessed with. Your Peninnah may feel like a curse at the moment, but they're actually your building block to your blessings. Peninnah is there to develop you into the Christian that you wouldn't have become on your own. After you obtain your heart's desire, send them a note saying, "Thanks for all you've done"!

# BLESSED BUT BROKE: WEEK 6 CHALLENGE

## Add To Your Retirement Account

Just because you're getting older doesn't mean you're getting closer to retirement. Retirement is a dollar amount, not an age. If you haven't already, start your retirement account. If you have one, add the maximum amount you possibly can. If your employer doesn't offer you one, then select your own retirement plan through a bank or brokerage. If your job does offer retirement, contribute the matching amount at minimum.

Identify your ideal retirement situation, and strive toward reaching it. Your "Golden Years" can start as soon as you have enough gold! Many people are so focused on today's financial struggle that they never plan for their future, and this is why they're still working! Don't let this be you!

# DAY 43: KING ME

*". . .that we also may be like all the nations, and that our king may judge us and go out before us and fight our battles"*
*-1 Samuel 8:20*

Samuel had served the children of Israel as Judge and Prophet for years and was growing old in age as Israel wanted new leadership. Samuel made his two sons judges over Israel, but they didn't serve Israel in honest ways: "But his son's did not walk in his ways; they turned aside after dishonest gain, took bribes, and perverted justice" (1 Sam. 8:3). The sons of Samuel, Joel and Abijah, allowed money to ruin their character and their reputation. As a Christian, you should never allow your character to be for sale regardless of how difficult your financial situation becomes. Even if you're not in financial hardship, don't allow greed to usher you out of the favor of God. The elders of Israel gathered with Samuel and used Joel and Abijah's tarnished reputations as part of the reason they wanted a new king (1 Sam. 8:4). The elders told Samuel they wanted a king to judge them like all the other nations (1 Sam. 8:5). The elders of Israel were about to allow their desire to be like everyone else to be their downfall. So many people are struggling financially because they want to be like everyone else.

But, when you are building your life in and on purpose, you live your life differently. Your integrity won't allow you to commit immoral acts for a quick dollar. When you have accepted generational wealth as a part of your life's vision you don't do what most people do with their money. Most people will see having a budget as a source of restriction, thinking of all the things they can't do. You need to see having a budget as a plan—a simple arrangement on where to guide your money. Most people will see a surplus of cash as a way to enjoy their present day moment. This is why their savings are constantly depleted, and they're always complaining about not having any money. You should see a surplus of cash as a normal everyday matter. View it as a source of raw material to build your financial future. Most people will see borrowing as a way to have instant gratification. You should count the entire cost, not just the minimum payments, and weigh all of your options before jumping into new debt. You must realize that sometimes instant gratification with your money can lead to future financial heartaches. Israel would have the instant pleasure of having a king like all nations, but they were empowering their future oppression.

Samuel tried to warn them by telling them the words of the Lord, but they refused to accept them (1 Sam. 8:19). The elders of Israel were so emotionally connected to being like all the other nations that they were not thinking logically. This is the same principle that so many other people use with their finances today. They place emotions such as feeling happy in the present over the logic of building long-term generational wealth. Just because you accepted Christ as Lord and Savior doesn't excuse you from being fiscally responsible. When you decide to be like all other nations with your financial decisions, you will suffer the same fate. The majority of working class adults live paycheck to paycheck and doesn't have at least $1,000 saved. That's not a nation you should strive to be like. You give power to the very systems that keep you financially oppressed when you spend the same as everyone else. Israel was supposed to be set apart rather than a replica of all nations. Set the trends of building generational wealth; don't follow the trends leading to poverty.

# DAY 44: PREPARE FOR WAR

*"Now there was no blacksmith to be found throughout all the land of Israel, for the Philistines said, 'Lest the Hebrews make swords or spears.'" -1 Samuel 13:19*

Saul had been King over Israel per the nation's request for two years when he attacked Philistine troops in Geba. Saul had three thousand men of Israel, two thousand for himself and another one thousand for his son Jonathan (1 Sam. 13:2). It had been tradition before going into battle to seek the Lord through prayer, worship, and offering a sacrifice. This was how Israel received their instructions, strategy, and favor from the Lord for their battles. Saul did none of this; Saul didn't execute effective leadership as their King but instead practiced impatience. Once the Philistines caught wind of this attack, they responded with thirty thousand chariots and six thousand horsemen (1 Sam. 13:5). When Israel saw the multitude of the Philistines, Israel scattered from the danger that was before them. The men of Israel hid in pits, rocks, caves, holes, and some of them even crossed back over the Jordan (1 Sam. 13:6-7). When Saul saw his troops scattered in fear, he finally decided to offer a burnt sacrifice to the Lord. After these events the Lord used the prophet Samuel to instruct Saul that his kingdom would no longer continue (1 Sam. 13:14).

Once the day of battle came the men of Israel didn't have any swords or spears to fight the Philistines (1 Sam. 13:22). A blacksmith was nowhere to be found within all of the Land of Israel (1 Sam. 13:19). The Bible teaches us that there is a danger in dependency on others for our own livelihood. This same principle applies to us in the area of our personal finances. How many people do you know who share employment with coworkers they don't like on a job they have grown to hate, yet that is their only source of income to provide for themselves and their family? You must ensure that your source of income is not dependent upon someone you view as an enemy. Israel had to depend on their Philistine oppressors to sharpen the tools they needed to grow and harvest the very food they depended on for life. Remember there aren't grocery stores that Israel could run to for their food. Israel could not sharpen and develop the very tools they needed to live on. You must be able to develop and sharpen the way you generate income without being dependent on someone else.

If you haven't already, you need focus on developing more than one source of income. Use your current income to buy other assets that will produce more income for you and your family. What happens to you and your loved ones if you lose your only source of income? Personal development should always be a priority in your life, develop the areas in which you are weak. If this were the case with Israel, they would have learned how to work with metal. The oppressor will never give the education that's needed for freedom. In this day and age of low wages, financial freedom is something you will have to earn. If you have one source of income that may only pay you just enough to cover the basics of life, it's solely on you to change your financial situation to build generational wealth. There are many unhealthy relationships that continue/ aren't ended because of finances. How many people deal with physical, verbal, and emotional abuse because they aren't financially prepared to leave? Don't allow a manager, family member, or the lack of money to keep you oppressed. Develop whatever skills you are lacking to increase the income needed to finance your freedom. Don't rob yourself and your family of becoming the person God intended for you to be by remaining in oppression.

# DAY 45: ALMOST THERE

*"Then Samuel took the horn of oil and anointed him in the midst of his brothers; and the Spirit of the Lord came upon David from that day forward. So Samuel arose and went to Ramah" -1 Samuel 16:13*

God had reached the point where He regretted making Saul King of Israel because of his disobedience (1 Sam. 15:10). Saul had repeatedly broken commandments and put his own self-interest above his duties as King of Israel. The true greatness of any leader is measured by their ability to serve and develop others. Saul was instructed to attack Amalek and kill every living and breathing being, but he didn't (1 Sam. 15:3). Saul decided to keep all of the best of Amalek livestock and spared the life of their leader, King Agag. Once the prophet Samuel confronted Saul, he initially denied being disobedient and eventually blamed other people for his acts of defiance (1 Sam. 15:24). As you strive to achieve greatness in your own life, always accept responsibility for your actions. Hold yourself accountable and never shift blame to anyone else for the decisions you make. Samuel told Saul that he was rejected from being King over Israel (1 Sam. 15:26). Samuel reached a breaking point and only went to see Saul on the day of his death (1 Sam. 15:35).

The anointing of David as King didn't look like royalty; it looked like tending sheep. It looked like long, hot, lonely, and sweaty days in the field tending to the animals. It looks like being underestimated by your own family. This also could hold true in your life: your current circumstances don't look like your future. The field is your place of preparation of what's to come in your life. When Samuel arrived at Jesse's house to anoint the new King of Israel, David wasn't even a consideration. David's father Jesse went down the line of seven of his eight sons, then Samuel brought David to mind (1 Sam. 16:11). Just because people have forgotten or even underestimate your abilities doesn't mean God has done so. You have greatness in you and your kingdom is coming, but it's beginning in a field. Maybe your current job doesn't seem to line up with your future, but know that it's preparing you for your greatness. Your present financial struggle is preparing you for the wealth that is to come. It's your ability to tend to the sheep that develop the servanthood needed for your kingdom. Use your time in the field to develop your abilities before your opportunity presents itself. It was in the field that David practiced his harp. It was David's ability to play the harp that placed him directly in Saul's presence.

Even after David was anointed as King, his role as Israel's leader wasn't immediate. You must also understand that what's inside of you will take time to manifest. You won't go from the field to the palace overnight. There could be years between the revelation of your destiny and the manifestation of your destiny. In this microwave society, we want everything quick, but God doesn't operate by self-imposed timelines and how you feel your life should look. As a society, we place too much value on how things appear to be. Tending to sheep in a field doesn't look as good as being ruler in the palace, but you will never arrive at your palace without managing your field properly. Saul's appearance was one of the reasons he was chosen as King but things are not always what they appear to be. As Christians we must remember God doesn't see as man sees. You might currently see yourself in lack; God sees you in abundance, and God is using your struggle to develop you into the person you need to be to have dominion over what's to come in your future.

# DAY 46: FACE YOUR GOLIATH

*"And Saul said to David, 'You are not able to go against this Philistine to fight with him; for you are a youth, and he a man of war from his youth.'" -1 Samuel 17:33*

The Bible teaches us that there was a Philistine named Goliath who was a champion man of war since his youth. Goliath is believed to have been over nine feet tall, weighing over four hundred pounds, and adorned with hundreds of pounds of armor in battle. Not only was Goliath big in physical stature, but he also had a big mouth. He verbally taunted the children of Israel and repeatedly welcomed them to battle. Many people today are facing their own Goliath who seems unbeatable, but instead of a man, it's financial hardship that's the giant. Goliath struck fear into all the children of Israel—everyone except young David. Just like David knew he would have victory over Goliath, you need to know you'll have victory over your financial struggles. You must possess one of the same traits that David used against Goliath, which was focus. David didn't focus on Goliath's size or résumé of war; he focused on the fact that this was an enemy coming against the God of Israel. You must not focus on how bad your finances are, but focus on the fact that with the right actions you will have victory over financial struggle.

By this time, David had been anointed King of Israel, but he was still working in the palace and as a shepherd before his battle with Goliath. David is teaching us that before you can arrive at your future you must take care of your present. You might be called to management or to full-time entrepreneurship, but you may not currently be in either of those positions. You must take care of today by working as hard as you possibly can at your current level. So many people are so focused on what their future holds that they neglect to maximize their present day. The future King of Israel arrived on the battlefield as a humble delivery boy. Jesse, David's father, asked him to deliver food to his brothers at their camp (1 Sam. 17:17). David's own brother reminded him that he was a shepherd and accused him of being a spectator (1 Sam. 17:28). Just like David, you are not called to be a witness; you are called to be a warrior. Don't be someone who operates in fear, constantly complains, and accepts what life gives you. Face your opposition of financial struggle and fight for the wealth God has in store for you.

You must not minimize your present position. It was David's background of tending sheep that prepared him to defeat Goliath. David had previously killed a lion and a bear and that experience made him consider Goliath simply as just another animal that needed to be put down (1 Sam 17:35). David didn't over complicate things by focusing on Goliath's size or using Saul's armor. You must not complicate your financial hardship by focusing on all of your areas of lack. While you are improving your finances, choose one task at a time. Focus on one task until it's completed, and then move on to the next task. David focused one stone at the forehead of Goliath, knocking him down and then moved to the next task of using the giant's own sword to cut his head off. David didn't use all of his five stones in hopes that one would connect; he was specific with his weapon and his target. You must also be specific with your money and your financial goals. When it was time for battle, David hurried, without procrastination, and ran to meet the Philistine (1 Sam. 17:48). You must no longer prolong taking the necessary steps needed to improve your financial conditions. David defeating Goliath inspired Israel to get off the sidelines and pursue the Philistines. You defeating financial struggles will also encourage others to do the same thing, so get off the sidelines of life and pursue the wealth that God has for you.

# DAY 47: PEOPLE PLEASING

*"So the women sang as they danced, and said: "Saul has slain his thousands, And David his ten thousands" -1 Samuel 18:7*

The same David who was underestimated by his own family and only viewed as a field servant had just slain the most feared Philistine in all the land. David went from being an unknown shepherd to a giant killer in seemingly the blink of an eye. In spite of all his newfound attention and praise, David remained humble. David's main focus was an audience of one—
the God of Israel. On the other hand, Saul lived for the attention, affection, and admiration of the people of Israel. Many people today are living with that same issue of placing too high of a value on other people's opinions. As you are building your generational wealth, you must be very cautious of seeking the praises of other people. You will not get the same public affection from other people building wealth, as you would displaying your wealth. The Bible teaches us that David behaved wisely when he was with Saul (1 Sam. 18:5). If you are going to become a landlord, business owner, or millionaire, you are going to have to behave wisely. Seek

to make wise decisions concerning your finances over seeking the approval of other people.

People currently own houses and cars that they truly can't afford only to give the impression of having wealth. People with real wealth will not put their money on display for the approval of other people. Broke people will remain broke when they decide to spend all of their income to impress other broke people. Don't allow social media and the praises of other people to delay you in building generational wealth. Don't spend your money trying to look like money. This action will only keep you in financial struggle. Don't get a new car payment; instead, invest that would-be car note for a return on your money. Place that $500 per month into an S&P 500 low-cost index fund. Instead of taking that vacation out of the country, stay local and use the difference to pay off more debt. Rather than eating out so much, start cooking more at home and use the money you save to build an investment account for your kid(s). Saul was consistently seeking the approval of other people over the approval of God. Saul's need to be admired by people eventually would lead to his demise. Don't allow the approval of the people in your life to lead you into bankruptcy.

David was in the palace to serve, but Saul allowed the opinions of others to destroy their relationship. Don't allow the opinions of broke people to destroy your relationship with money. Money is here to serve you not to be a ruler over you. Money rules over you when the decisions you make in life are always based on your available balance. "You work hard, enjoy your money now," "you're too young to think about retirement," and "you'll always have a car note" are all opinions that should hold no value in your life. Start using your income solely to build wealth and acquire assets rather than the praises of other people. David went from the field as a shepherd to the palace as a military leader, but he continued to live his life as a servant (1 Sam. 18:5). Just like David, as you grow in status and income, the way you live your life doesn't have to change. Just because your position and salary grows doesn't mean you have to change your life by increasing your expenses. So many people allow their expenses to grow as their compensation grows; don't let that be you. Your grandkids won't be able to live off of the praises you receive from being the best dressed. Don't place a high value on other people viewing you as a person with money. Be the person that places a high value on building generational wealth.

# DAY 48: BROTHERLY LOVE

*"And he said to him, 'Do not fear, for the hand of my father shall not find you. You shall be king over Israel, and I shall be next to you. Even my father Saul knows that.'"*
*-1 Samuel 23:17*

By this time, Saul had made several unsuccessful attempts to kill David and was now fully committed to taking his life. David hadn't committed any action to bring dishonor to the throne, but Saul was being guided by insecurities. Saul somehow thought that killing David would correct all of the consequences he had to face because of his bad decisions. He tried to correct his past mistakes by making more bad choices. While David was fleeing for his life, Jonathan the son of Saul, would turn out to become one of David's most loyal allies. Jonathan didn't have misplaced loyalty just because Saul was his father.

John Churton Collins said it best: "In prosperity our friends know us; in adversity we know our friends." Jonathan wasn't just there for David when things were going well; he was also there during difficulty. David went from living in the palace to living on the run, and Jonathan's loyalty never shifted. Some people are in your life only for what they can get out of you, especially when it comes to the area of finances. Nothing breaks up family, relationships, or employment like money. People with big hearts make for easy targets and must learn to do what's best not what's convenient. I'm sure it wasn't convenient for Jonathan to choose David over his own father Saul, but he did what was best. If you're quick to say yes and are always loyal to being the helping hand, you can easily find yourself being taken advantage of. So many people remain in relationships even though the loyalty is one-sided. A great relationship doesn't have just one person doing all of the work.

Don't allow anyone to use your loyalty as a weapon against you. You can't be loyal to someone to the point that it leads to your own demise. They might share the same blood and last name as you, but even family can lead to your demise. There are people out there who won't break a sweat for you yet continually want you to break your back for them. Take inventory of all the relationships in your life, and see who's truly loyal.

I've personally seen people go the extra mile with their loyalty to jobs that their family suffered. You can't be so loyal to your job that it costs you your family. Honor your wedding vows and growing kids more than your company mission statement and profit margins. Focus on building your finances up to the point that you won't have to tolerate any form of employment that asks you to be more loyal to the job more than your family.

Also, don't allow your family to guilt you into becoming a readily available ATM. There's a big difference between being a blessing and being an enabler. Jonathan gave David information and guidance but David was still the one who had to take action to apply that information. People who refuse to take action to improve their own situation(s) are people who don't deserve your loyalty. Misplaced loyalty can often require a price that you can't afford. Being loyal to the wrong people can cost you money, healthy relationships, and even your spouse. Jonathan was there for David in the palace, the battlefield, and the wilderness. Surround yourself with people who are loyal like Jonathan because you'll need them. Don't allow your desire to make people happy lead you or your family to your own demise. Loyalty should not be a dead end; it's a two-way street.

# DAY 49: RUNNING WITH PATIENCE

*"But David said to Abishai, 'Do not destroy him; for who can stretch out his hand against the Lord's anointed, and be guiltless.'"*
*-1 Samuel 26:9*

In order to protect his own life, David had to flee from Saul and make his new home in the caves of the wilderness. Saul attempted to use his daughter as a snare for David by which he would die by the hands of the Philistines in battles (1 Sam. 18:21). Saul also tried to kill his own Son, Jonathan for helping David escape (1 Sam. 20:33). While on the run, David was able to find food in the city of Nob from the priest Ahimelech (1 Sam 21:6). And because they assisted David in his fleeing, Saul had Ahimelech and the other priest of the Lord killed. Saul was fully committed to killing David and anyone who helped David. For their own safety, David even had to have his family relocated to Moab to protect them from Saul (1 Sam. 22:3-4). David was living in the wilderness, separated from his family, and had thousands of troops seeking to end his life. I'm sure this was not an easy cross to bear. The Bible teaches us that Saul sought David everyday but was unsuccessful (1 Sam. 23:14). Place yourself in David's shoes for a moment: would you desire for this season of your life to be over? I know I would!

While David and his men were hiding in a cave, Saul came in to attend to his needs and that provided an opportunity for David to end Saul's pursuit by taking his life (1 Sam. 24:3). David, however, exercised restraint and only cut off a corner of his robe and even that troubled him (1 Sam. 24:5). At that moment David exercised the principle of delayed gratification, and this is something we must exercise in the area of our finances. David exercised discipline and didn't kill Saul even though he had the opportunity to do so. You must exercise discipline and decide not to buy certain things just because you have a chance to do so. David would have jumped outside of the Will of God by killing Saul. So many people go outside of the Will of God to accomplish a desired result and then call it a blessing. God wouldn't bless you with a car with a twenty percent interest rate. God doesn't bless you with a house that requires you to work overtime just to make the minimum payment due for the mortgage. God doesn't bless us with liabilities that have high interest rates and payment plans attached.

You should not rush the process of achieving a desired financial result. This action will often lead you into debt and future financial hardship. Not practicing delayed gratification is a guaranteed way to have you drowning in debt. Don't rush the process by financing things you can't afford to buy. Delayed gratification doesn't start when your desire starts; it starts once you are actually in a position to take action. Spending money provides instant gratification with no future return on your money spent. Investing money requires delayed gratification while your investment grows to provide you a return on your money spent. If David could practice delayed gratification with his life on the line, surely you can exercise discipline with your money on the line. David would eventually have a second chance to kill Saul, but he opted only to take his spear and water jug (1 Sam. 26:12). If you are going to build generational wealth, you are going to have to exercise discipline more than just one time. Delayed gratification is a habit that's going to have to be repeated as you acquire your assets. People who are not focused on building wealth will always find ways to spend and enjoy their money in the moment. Like David, don't rush your process but wait on the Lord for your divine time for manifestation.

# BLESSED BUT BROKE: WEEK 7 CHALLENGE

## Start A Stock Brokerage Account

Buying stocks isn't as hard as it once was. I personally invest in *index funds,* which is where you buy a certain group of stocks instead of particular ones. The compound interest is what you're after. This is where your money makes you more money over time. Compound interest is a great protector against inflation, which is where the value of your dollar drops over time. This is why the prices for goods and services keep going up.

I recommend that you read this book called *The Little Book of Common Sense Investing* by John Bogle. This is a great book to increase your stock investing knowledge.

# DAY 50: ZION NOT ZIKLAG

*"So Achish gave him Ziklag that day. Therefore Ziklag has belonged to the kings of Judah to this day." -1 Samuel 27:6*

To avoid losing his life by the hand of Saul, David took himself and his men and decided to make his home in the land of the Philistines. David had already taken the life of their prized champion Goliath and had killed numerous Philistine soldiers. The Philistines granted David and his six hundred men the county of Ziklag to call home (1 Sam. 27:6). The circumstances for David and his men had improved. He no longer had to flee from Saul, the wilderness was no longer his home, and they increased their possessions. David led Achish, the Philistine king of Gath, to believe that he and his men were raiding places in Israel, but the truth was David was actually making raids in other Philistine countries. That's right, while living in Ziklag under the Philistines, David was also killing them and taking their possessions as his own. There's a saying, "never let a good crisis go to waste." And I say this to you: never let a good financial struggle go to waste. When you have a less than ideal opportunity to improve your circumstances, this is your own personal Ziklag experience.

Maybe you have to get a part-time job to improve your financial situation, something that might be less than ideal. Or maybe you have to move in with family to save on your housing expenses. You might have to remain in your current work environment, even though it's working your last nerve, in order to provide for your family. You might have to continue to drive your car with no air and the check engine light on in order to build your savings. David's destiny wasn't to remain in Ziklag, David was called to be king of Israel. Like David, your destiny isn't to remain amongst your enemies. Don't allow your current situations to make you lose heart in what God has called you to fulfill. David had chosen to use his time in Ziklag to be productive and not complain about how bad things were. So many people waste so much time complaining about their situations that they never make the time to improve their circumstances. This is one of the reasons why people remain in their personal Ziklag for so long. Some people will allow a temporary improvement in circumstances to cause them to no longer strive to develop personally, professionally, or spiritually.

Although David received refuge from Saul, he couldn't rule all of Israel living in Ziklag. You shouldn't allow a temporary improvement in circumstances to prevent you from reaching your destiny. There's no such thing as good enough when God has called you to greater. David was in Ziglak from a total of sixteen months before leaving, but maybe you've been in Ziklag for years.

Obtaining a small win can feel good after many years of struggle; however, your goal as a Christian is not only about receiving pleasure but also it's about achieving purpose. Ziklag was the place where David avoided his threat of the pursuit from Saul. Use your Ziklag to eliminate your biggest threat but don't lose sight of your palace. Your palace is the destiny that God has called you to fulfill. The amount of success you strive for will always be greater than the amount of success you settle for. Even though you might be facing tremendous adversity, identify the ways you can still be productive. David and his men weren't just sitting idle while in Ziklag. Don't use your struggle as an excuse to avoid personal development and cause you to grow bitter. Find refuge from your temporary difficulty and use that relief to become the best version of yourself that you can be.

# DAY 51: CRY A RIVER

*"Then David and the people who were with him lifted up their voices and wept, until they had no more power to weep." -1 Samuel 30:4*

David and his men left Ziklag to join the Philistines in battle against Saul and the people of Israel. But before they could depart for battle, David and his men were rejected for duty by the princes of the Philistines (1 Sam. 29:4). God used the princes' mistrust of David to prevent him from taking part in the battle that would take the life of Saul and his sons. David and his men returned to their home in Ziklag only to find out that it had been invaded and burned with fire (1 Sam. 30:1). The Amalekites were behind the attack on Ziklag and they had taken captive all the people and taken great spoils of the land. All the possessions and family that David and his men had gained in the wilderness and Ziklag had now been lost. David's troops were so grieved that they spoke of stoning him (1 Sam. 30:6). These are the same men who were willing to live in the wilderness and also die for him. The pain of losing something that's yours often cuts you deeply and changes you. Even though David and his men were in a very emotional place, David didn't respond emotionally. David went to the ultimate source of strength for guidance on his next move.

Instead of an invasion, maybe you have lost money for yourself and the ones you love from a business investment that didn't work out, and maybe that business ruined your credit. Most businesses have a high rate of failure within their first year. Maybe you've experience losing your home through eviction or foreclosure. Watching someone getting kicked out of their home is a very ugly and painful thing to see. Or maybe you've lost your car because of repossession from non-payment on your car loan. With eight out of ten Americans living paycheck-to-paycheck, getting behind on your bills and losing your possessions is a very real possibility. Maybe you were even terminated from a job that you loved and became unemployed. Like David, the first thing you should do after loss is to seek guidance from the Lord. God told David to pursue the Amalekites and recover everything without fail (1 Sam. 30:8). Losing something that you cherish can lead to depression and make you feel like a failure. In your own personal pursuit of recovery, it's very critical that you don't take that mindset of failure. Remember failure is a system that didn't work; it's not your identity. The opportunity to recover is a blessing; take full advantage of it.

David came across an Egyptian who was a servant of the Amalekites who had grown sick and had been left for dead in a field (1 Sam 30:11). God used David to bless the Egyptian with food and preserve his life, and He used the Egyptian to bless David by leading him and his men right to the Amalekites. The Bible is teaching us that even in the midst of your loss, God is still in the blessing business. David attacked the Amalekites and recovered all that was lost while the Amalekites were celebrating from twilight to evening (1 Sam 30:17). If you have experienced loss in an area of your life, you too can recover all that was lost. You can rebuild your credit and recover money lost from investments that didn't go as planned. You can get a new home, a new job, or a new vehicle as long as you're willing to pursue recovery. David had two hundred troops that remained behind in Ziklag and could not bring themselves to join him in their fight for recovery. You won't be able to recover any of your lost possessions as long as you're choosing to remain in your heartache and misery. Don't allow experiencing loss to force you into a state of paralysis. Allow experiencing loss to force you into a state of pursuit.

# DAY 52: GIVE IT TIME

*"Now there was a long war between the house of Saul and the house of David. But David grew stronger and stronger, and the house of Saul grew weaker and weaker." -2 Samuel 3:1*

It's important for you to remember that David wasn't born a fierce warrior, but he was a shepherd. David wasn't born into the royal family, but he was developed into it. David wasn't out networking when he was anointed as king, but he was tending sheep. David's family wasn't his strongest support system, and they consistently belittled and underestimated him. It wasn't David's amount of wealth that got him into the palace under the king; it was his ability to play the harp. The relationship between Saul and David began in mentorship, but it ended in attempted murder. It was David's response to life's adversities that developed him into the leader God created him to be. David was anointed as king as a teenager but didn't receive his crown until he was thirty years old (2 Sam. 5:4). David faced and obtained victory over numerous challenges for over a decade. David's life was a series of battles that he was blessed to conquer. You will not be able to enjoy the spoils of war without a fight. David is teaching us that your calling does not grant you a life free of conflict.

More than likely you were not born into a family of wealth, but you're going to have to create it. The favor of God in your life will always be greater than any of your shortcomings. You can come from a background of poverty and still reach millionaire status. On your pursuit of building generational wealth, you will have some Sauls in your life. Your Sauls may not try to physically kill you, but they will try to kill the dreams inside of you. David didn't obtain the throne overnight, and you won't reach generational wealth overnight. Tyler Perry stated: "It took me twenty years to become an overnight success." Track athletes train for the Olympics for four years just for a ten to twenty second race. Professional athletes celebrate on draft night, but it was their level of practice that led them there. The victory of war is determined by a series of battles, not just one fight. You more than likely won't build generational wealth overnight, over a month, or in your first year. Commitment to improving your finances shouldn't be looked at as only a short-term goal. Focus on the complete management of your money, not just your salary from your job. High-income earners also live paycheck-to-paycheck because income alone doesn't equal wealth.

After the death of Saul and his sons, David still yet wasn't the king of Israel. Before he took office as the king of Israel, he was anointed as the King of Judah. Judah was the area south of Israel. A son named Ishbosheth survived Saul, and he would be chosen to be king of Israel. This was how the house of Saul and the house of David were formed. This was another hurdle that David had to clear. On your road to building generational wealth, you will face multiple challenges, but don't allow these obstacles to get you off the path of building your wealth. David's house grew over time while Saul's house grew weaker because of the response to adversity. Like David, you need to exercise wisdom over the course of years if you are to fulfill your destiny. Quick results are results that normally don't last long. Ishbosheth only reigned for two years and David would reign for over thirty years. Even though it doesn't feel good, don't rush the process. Your response to adversity is developing the muscle memory you'll need once you take office. Building wealth is a series of battles, and it's a long process. Process comes before promise in the dictionary and also with God.

# DAY 53: KEEP GOING

*"So David knew that the Lord had established him as king over Israel, and that He had exalted His kingdom for the sake of His people Israel" -2 Samuel 5:12*

What do you do when you finally achieve the position that required years of your life and much adversity to reach it? David responded to the fulfillment of his achievement by continuing to complete more tasks. David's first official act as king of Israel was taking possession of the stronghold city of Zion (2 Sam. 5:7). Even after years of difficulty and numerous battles, David didn't decide to go on vacation. Your future success is often based on how you handle your present success. Oftentimes people will allow their achievements to cause them to grow unmotivated and lazy. You must develop and continue the habit of achievement amnesia. This is where people continue to focus on and improve upon the actions and processes of achievement while not dwelling long on a particular result. David didn't focus on the fact that he obtained his long awaited crown; he, instead, started construction. Don't allow your success at reaching some of your goals to stop you from building toward other goals. This is especially true when it comes to the area of personal finances. Satisfaction often leads people to complacency, and being complacent towards your money can often lead to financial hardship. You must do as David and continue to build.

The Philistines went up in search for David once they heard that he was anointed king of Israel (2 Sam. 5:17). The Bible is teaching us that the crown didn't free David from confrontation. The Bible is also showing you that success often attracts enemies that would like to halt your growth. Envy, jealousy, and insecurities will commonly lead your haters to their own demise without a direct response from you, but the best way to handle opposition from those who are against you is to seek guidance from the Lord. David was a seasoned warrior and no stranger to battle, but he didn't respond to the Philistines without direct instruction from God. Receiving instructions before committing to any actions will often lead to better outcomes. Unsatisfied with their first defeat, the Philistines decided to come against David once more and David yet again responded by receiving instructions from God. David was instructed to begin the attack by circling behind the Philistines (2 Sam. 5:23). David's crown or previous victory still didn't hinder him from humbling himself and seeking instruction, and you must apply this same principle of always seeking instructions.

I, personally, witnessed this with the sale of my first book, One Paycheck At A Time, on the value that different people placed on instruction. The people I personally knew who needed the information the most were the slowest and least likely to buy; however, the people who were in better financial situations than most were the quickest and first to buy. It's difficult for people to create value in their life when they don't value instruction. There's a reason why the biggest houses often have the biggest personal libraries. Not having the right information will always keep people experiencing hardship. Your prior success shouldn't guide you from continuing to consistently seek instruction. David's placement as king wasn't just about him, but it was about all of Israel. And you improving and building your finances doesn't just affect you: think about all the people to whom you can be a blessing. Instruction is oftentimes free, but construction has a cost. You might have enough money for you and your family, but don't allow that to prevent you from continuing to build wealth that can benefit others.

# DAY 54: ROUGH BEGINNINGS

*"Then David comforted Bathsheba his wife, and went in to her and lay with her. So she bore a son, and he called his name Solomon. Now the Lord loved him." -2 Samuel 12:24*

The life you experience doesn't have to be the sum total of the conditions that you were born into. Your greatness will be rooted in the decisions and actions you make, not the actions of your family. If you were born into a dysfunctional family, your kids and grandkids don't have to share the same testimony. While it may be difficult, don't allow the conditions surrounding your family to stop you from achieving greatness. Much of the brokenness we face as adults started from the adversity we experienced during childhood. Some people can never experience a healthy relationship because they were never exposed to one growing up. There's a test that measures the likelihood of people repeating the same struggles they grew up in called the Adverse Childhood Experiences (ACE) test. The ACE model that teaches the higher the score the more likely the cycle of adversity will be repeated. If you were born into poverty, you have a greater chance of a high ACE score. If anyone had a reason not to strive for greatness because of their family, it was Solomon. And there's no doubt in my mind that Solomon would have received a high ACE score.

King David was at home during the time kings normally go out to battle (2 Sam. 11:1). David noticed a beautiful woman taking a bath and inquired about her (2 Sam. 11:3). It turned out that this beautiful woman was married to Uriah the Hittite, one of David's most loyal and fiercest warriors. Not only did David get Uriah's wife Bathsheba pregnant, David also had Uriah killed and took Bathsheba as his own wife (2 Sam. 12:9). Their union birthed Solomon. Betrayal, adultery, and murder were the circumstances in which Solomon's parents' union began. The dysfunction of Solomon's family did not end at his parents: Solomon had a brother named Amnon, and they shared a sister named Tamar. Amnon wanted to lay with his own sister so badly that he became ill and started losing weight (2 Sam. 13:4). Amnon had a friend named Jonadab, whom instructed Amnon on how to rape his sister Tamar (2 Sam. 13:5). Solomon's brother Absalom would avenge his sister's death by killing Amnon two years later. Absalom's thirst for blood wouldn't stop at killing his brother; however, Absalom also sought to overtake David as the new king of Israel by attempting to have his father killed (2 Sam 17:2). Absalom's thirst for blood would eventually lead him to his own death (2 Sam. 18:15). These were the unique individuals whom Solomon would call family.

Regardless of your parents' circumstances during your conception, you were born for a purpose. Your identity and experiences in life shouldn't be based on what your parents did or didn't do. You are not responsible for the conditions you are born into, but you are responsible for your life and the conditions your kids are born into. The role of a parent is to ensure that their kid(s) can experience a childhood they don't need to recover from. Despite all of this madness between his family members, Solomon would become king and not just any king, but he would become the wisest and richest king of all time. Your sanity and mental health should be a priority in your life: there's no shame in having your pastor and your therapist. Money can purchase a lot of things, but it can't buy you healing. Seek the Lord, mentorship, and professional counseling if you have pain too great to deal with on your own. While building generational wealth, you are also charged with making different generational choices and breaking generational curses.

# DAY 55: TIRED BOSS

*"When the Philistines were at war again with Israel, David and his servants with him went down and fought against the Philistines; and David grew faint" -2 Samuel 21:15*

What will you do when your body tells you it's time to slow down, and you can't physically perform like you used to? David had been fighting in battles since he was a teenager, but his body began responding differently once he became an older man. David has reached a point where his responsibility as leader could no longer be on the battlefield as a warrior. Fatigue almost cost David his life as the Philistine Ishbi-Benob almost killed him, but Abishai, one of the "Mighty Men," came to David's aid and killed the Philistine (2 Sam 21:17). David's men stated, "You shall go out no more with us to battle, lest you quench the lamp of Israel" (2 Sam 21:17). The word quench, in this context, means to extinguish. David's men knew that he could no longer physically fight, but Israel was still dependent upon him. David's men were already trained and battle-tested before he reached his older age and could no longer fight. What do you currently have in place that will generate your income when you no longer have the mental desire or physical will to work? The best time to consider and prepare your options is now.

Always remember that retirement is not a certain age, but rather it's a certain dollar amount. A good rule of thumb is to take your desired annual income and multiply that by twenty-five. For example, for a $60,000 annual income will require a savings of 1.5 million. Your required savings number shouldn't scare you. Remember David didn't start with Goliath: he started with smaller animals that came against his sheep (1 Sam. 17:35). Start at your current level and focus on building your wealth from wherever you might be. If you also decide to follow Warren Buffett's advice and open a **Low Cost S&P 500 Index Fund** account, one of your best friends will be compound interest, which is when the interest you've previously made generates its own interest. For example, you make an investment that pays ten percent on an annual basis, which is an almost average return on this type of account. If you start with $1,000, it becomes $1,100 because of the interest made. Now your $1,100 becomes $1,210 after 2 years. This is money that your money is making without you physically having to go to battle for it. In the battle for generational wealth, you must turn your money into soldiers that recruit other soldiers.

When you waste money, you also waste the return that money could have generated. Keep this in mind as you're shopping online and eating out. That money that appears to be small can be the difference between poverty and wealth. Paying rent is another big money waster as it doesn't allow for you to build equity, which is the difference between what you owe on a property and what the property is worth. You will always need a place to live; ownership allows for you to grow your wealth while keeping a roof over your head. If your current credit score doesn't allow for you to qualify, do what needs to be done to improve your score. When you use bad credit as an excuse to keep renting, you're building wealth for another family to enjoy. Frivolous spending prevents most people from building their wealth and you shouldn't be one of them. There's going to come a point at which you can no longer physically work, but this won't free you from certain financial obligations. Start preparing for your retirement before you grow faint. You weren't created to spend all of your years battling for money. Grow your wealth and assets to the point where they do the battling for you, and, unlike humans, your money doesn't get tired and grow faint.

# DAY 56: CHOOSE WISDOM

*"And I have also given you what you have not asked: both riches and honor, so that there shall not be anyone like you among the kings all your days." -1 Kings 3:13*

If God came to you tonight and said, "Ask! What shall I give you?" How would you respond to this question? King Solomon responded by asking for an understanding heart to judge God's people (1 Kgs 3:9). God blessed King Solomon with wisdom and an understanding heart with pleasure. As a bonus, God also gave him riches and honor. King Solomon is believed to have been around twenty years old around the time of this dream and prayer. King Solomon was young but he was mature enough to seek wisdom. In personal finance and in all other areas of your life, you should remain in a constant state of seeking wisdom. Wisdom is part of the foundation in which all areas of our lives should be built upon. The wisest and richest king ever didn't pray for money; he prayed for wisdom. King Solomon shows that obtaining wisdom comes before obtaining wealth. Creating income only requires a job, but creating wealth will require wisdom. As you work to build your available balance, also work toward building your available knowledge.

Make learning a priority in your life and promote consistent learning to the ones you love. Learning shouldn't stop just because you've obtained a diploma or degree; instead, learning and growing in wisdom should be a lifestyle habit. Oftentimes the people who struggle the most are the ones who learn the least. As an African American man, I hate to hear other African Americans say, "I don't like to read." The reason is because black people were once mutilated and executed for learning how to read. You now have the option of eBooks and audiobooks to grow your knowledge in any area. Ignorance is the gatekeeper of struggle, hardship, and captivity, and, for most, it's also a personal choice. Some people will travel to a completely different state to enjoy a good meal, spend an entire weekend on their television watching entire seasons of shows, and spend hours scrolling through social media because they are bored. Time shouldn't be wasted on boredom when there's wealth that needs to be built. These are just some examples of time that could be otherwise dedicated to growing your knowledge in a certain area.

King Solomon wouldn't have been as effective at leading and growing the children of Israel without wisdom and humility. In order for you to learn anything, you must accept the fact that you don't know something. Some people have so much pride that it prevents them from learning new things. Solomon was in the highest position in Israel as their King yet humble enough to call himself a little child (1 Kgs 3:7). Regardless of your current age or title, there's always something for you to learn and people to learn from. Seek quality mentorship from people who only want the best from you. People who've obtained success in the areas that you are seeking to grow in: people who don't make the commitment to grow in wisdom concerning finances will always have their income determined by someone else. It's a shame that so many people experiencing financial hardship always seem to find money for everything except investing in themselves. Always remember, before King Solomon walked in prosperity, he walked in wisdom. One of the best investments you can make to grow your money is to grow your knowledge about money. The money you have available will always be based upon the same amount of wisdom you choose to exercise concerning your money.


187

# BLESSED BUT BROKE: WEEK 8 CHALLENGE

## Last Will & Testament

This is a document that will help to prevent a lot of unnecessary conflict among your family members. If you haven't done so already, make the time to establish a living will. I definitely want you to build wealth for your family, but I also want you to direct your wealth before you transition. I know from experience how the fight for personal possessions can break families apart. Don't allow this to be your family.

# DAY 57: BE THE BEST

*"Now therefore, command that they cut down cedars for me from Lebanon; and my servants will be with your servants, and I will pay you wages for your servants according to whatever you say. For you know there is none among us who has the skill to cut timber like the Sidonians". -1 Kings 5:6*

Being the best in a specialized field will oftentimes provide you with an opportunity to experience prosperity; however, being an average worker in any field usually leads to average money. And with six out of ten working adults not having $1,000 saved, average money commonly amounts to having no money. You should strive to be the best in your work and life while avoiding being average at all cost. Solomon wasn't your average king; he was the best to ever do it. People from all walks of life came to seek the Wisdom of Solomon (1 Kgs 4:34). Solomon didn't manage his kingdom in an average manner, and you shouldn't manage your finances in an average manner. Average money management will lead you to average money, and average money equals broke. Being the best will always provide you with opportunities that being average would never be able to produce.

Solomon didn't use just any trees available; he purchased the cedar wood from Lebanon because it was known for being the best. Solomon also told King Hiram of Tyre that his servants would be paid according to whatever Hiram said. When you are the best at what you do, you don't have to ask for a discount or payment plan options. Being the best places you in a position to pay the asking price in full, and when you're the best at what you do, there's no discount in your salary. There's always someone willing to pay top dollar for high quality work, products, and services. Your current quality of life is a direct reflection of your previous ability to operate in excellence or "averageness." Solomon stated that there was none among them who had a skill to cut timber like the Sidonians (1 Kgs 5:6). What skill set do you possess that others will pay you top dollar to perform? Having a skill that you can perform at a high level creates a demand for your talents, and being in demand places a high value on your skillset and creates more opportunity for income. Excellence affords you the opportunity to name your price, not negotiate your price.

The average person doesn't focus on development and creation; this is why they remain average. They accept things as they are, rather than as what they could become. People who operate in excellence will always focus on how to improve in order to become the best version of themselves. Solomon could have just rested on the fact that he was king, but because he wanted to become the best, he prayed for wisdom. Don't allow temporary financial hardship to be an excuse for you to perform at an average level. Your prayers and your work ethic directed toward your goals don't cost money: the amount of effort you put toward being the best is determined by your mindset, not what you can afford. Operating at an average level places you in the passenger seat of wealth building because someone else is determining your income; however, operating in excellence places you in the driver's seat of creating your generational wealth. Don't rob yourself and the ones you love of the opportunity to experience the best version of you. Zig Ziglar stated: "You don't have to be great to start, but you have to start to be great." Start today by putting forth your absolute best effort in every area of your life.

# DAY 58: MULTIPLE STREAMS

*"So King Solomon surpassed all the kings of the Earth in riches and wisdom."*
*-1 Kings 10:23*

King Solomon had the wisdom and favor of God in a mighty way. One of the ways Solomon applied this wisdom and grew in prosperity was by creating multiple streams of income. In today's society, multiple streams of income are a necessity. One source of income might be able to put a roof over your head and food on the table, but King Solomon is showing us that one of the keys to experiencing abundant prosperity is establishing more than one source of income. As King, Solomon received 666 talents of pure gold annually (1 Kgs 10:14). One talent weighed around seventy to seventy-five- pounds and you already know there's 16 ounces in one pound. At the time of this writing, gold is selling for $1,942 per ounce. So in today's money one talent of gold is equal to over 2 million dollars. Solomon was a billionaire based on his annual salary alone but didn't let his high salary stop him from creating multiple streams of income. Solomon's journey toward abundance started in prayer— the ideal starting point for all of us. Solomon's greatest asset was his wisdom, and he used that asset to create more assets. This is the concept of acquiring assets you need to apply in your own journey toward building generational wealth.

The Bible teaches us that King Solomon built up a labor force (1Kgs 9:15). In other words King Solomon created an organized system of passive income. Passive income is money that's generated for you that you don't physically trade time for dollars. Trading time for dollars will always be limited because you can only be in one place at a time, you may experience fatigue, and there are only twenty-four hours in a day. The wealthiest among us today all use some form of passive income and you should too. You can generate passive income from owning rental property, attained dividends from certain stocks you can buy, owning a business, or accruing interest from bonds. A bond is basically a loan that you provide to the government or a business that repays your principal money with interest. Solomon also entered the import/export business by building and using merchant ships. The ships were staffed with servants from King Hiram and King Solomon because King Hiram's servants knew the sea (1 Kgs 9:26). These ships went out on three-year voyages and returned with gold, silver, ivory, and animals (1Kgs 10:22). Solomon used the asset of ships to generate wealth outside of Israel, and you can use the asset of the internet to generate wealth on a national and global scale. Your ability to generate income is no longer limited to the area in which you live.

King Solomon was a highly sought after consultant by the everyday person to royalty. These consultations would often end in an offering. The Queen of Sheba gifted Solomon with spices, precious stones, and 120 talents of gold after meeting with him (1 Kgs 10:10). Solomon also used his resources to build and develop real estate outside of the Temple of God (1 Kgs 9:15). The precious metal of gold and real estate ownership are two assets that have held value since the Garden of Eden (Gen. 2:11). These are definitely assets that will assist you in the development of building generational wealth. Seek and apply wisdom to acquire great assets, and use the income of those assets to purchase more assets. The wisest and richest king to ever live understood the importance of multiple streams of income, and hopefully you do too. One is too dangerous and too small of a number to have for sources of income: multiple streams of income will provide you with multiple options in life. One source of income is a one-way street with financial struggle as its dead in.

# DAY 59: PILLOW TALK

*"For it was so, when Solomon was old, that his wives turned his heart after other gods; and his heart was not loyal to the Lord his God, as was the heart of his father David."*
*-1 Kings 11:4*

Heart Disease is the number one killer for adults living in the United States, and heart's desires are the number one killer for Christians serving in the Kingdom of God. The things you feed your physical body and your spirit will produce the reality you have to face. Giving into your vices can gradually or suddenly prevent you from fulfilling the vision God has placed in your heart. God warned Israel not to marry the unbelievers because they would lead Israel away from God (1 Kgs 11:2). Not only was Solomon led away, he also built and established temples for worship in high places for their pagan gods (1 Kgs 11:7). The need to experience pleasure should never be made a priority over your purpose. Whether it's drugs, cigarettes, alcohol, sex, or bad eating habits, everyone has a vice, but that doesn't mean you have to give into them. Giving into your vices often leaves you with a desire of wanting it more. Solomon was the richest king ever, but there's no amount of money that can free us from the consequences of the decisions we make, and those consequences affect us and the ones we love. God told Solomon that He would tear the kingdom out of his hand, thus impacting Solomon's descendants (1 Kgs 11:12).

Operating in lust can instantly damage a legacy that required years to build. Solomon's idolatry led to the demise of the kingdom he took decades to construct. David was a man after God's own heart, and Solomon was the wisest king ever; however, both of them allowed their desire to be their downfall. You don't have to be the wisest person ever to be smart enough to create distance between you and your vices. If your struggle is smoking, don't hang around smokers. If your struggle is unhealthy foods, stay away from drive-thrus. If you struggle with drinking, don't hang around people who like to drink. If sex is your struggle, avoid situations that can lead to sex outside of the boundaries of marriage. Solomon had the foreign ladies in his bed— he was too close to them. David was able to see Bathsheba bathing—he was too close to her. Don't be overconfident in your ability to fight temptation; instead, be strong enough to avoid temptation completely. The Bible teaches us that Solomon loved many foreign women, but experiencing a love that's ungodly only leads to heartbreak, regardless of your wealth (1 Kgs 11:1).

A heart divided against God leads to a weak heart and a weak spiritual foundation, and anything built on a weak foundation will eventually fail. Solomon didn't start with building high places to worship and sacrifice to these pagan gods; he started with lying with them. Like many other living creations, your thirst for those ungodly desires will grow as you nurture them. Growing our relationship with those who have our best interest in mind and who are loyal should always be a priority. Loyalty is a trait that's high in demand but low in supply in today's society. It was the God of Israel who gave Solomon the wisdom that he possessed. And Solomon repaid him in his old age by serving the gods of his foreign women. Solomon would eventually take a page out of Saul's book and attempt to kill the newly anointed king (1 Kgs 11:40). Don't allow things and people who are not of God to penetrate your heart and lead you away from God. The amount of money and wisdom you possess is useless if you're letting what's between your legs make your decisions.

# DAY 60: HEARING GOD'S VOICE

*"Then Elijah said to Ahab, 'Go up, eat and drink; for there is the sound of abundance of rain.'" -1 Kings 18:41*

You will not be able to purchase your way into heaven regardless of the amount of wealth you will build here on Earth, so in the midst of obtaining assets, don't allow your relationship with God to become your biggest liability. Your relationship with God can place you in circumstances that you won't be able to buy your way into, and this was the very case with God's prophet Elijah. God used the prophet Elijah to tell King Ahab that there would be no more rain, except at his word (1 Kgs 17:1). A drought during these days is equivalent to a modern-day recession. Because of his relationship with God, Elijah would know the starting and stopping point of this drought.

Being in a position to hear the directions of God is priceless and can be the difference between life and death. Your ability to hear the voice of God isn't based on your revenue but rather on your relationship. God instructed Elijah on exactly where to go throughout this drought that would end up lasting for over three years. Elijah's first stop would be by the brook cherith where God would use ravens to feed him (1 Kgs 17:6). Once that brook dried up because of the lack of rain, God directed Elijah to Zarephath. The Bible is teaching us that while our current environment may be out of resources, God never will be. Zarephath was the home of Jezebel and the capital city of pagan worship of the god Baal. The Lord used a widow in the city of Zarephath to provide for Elijah. Your relationship with God has to be solid for you to go into enemy territory tired, hungry, and weaponless and receive favor. The same holds true for this widow. She only had a handful of flour and a little oil in a jar as food to eat for herself and her son, but Elijah instructed her that if she fed him first that her food supply would not run out (1 Kgs 17:12, 13-14). She did according to what the prophet instructed her to do, and they were all able to eat for many days.

Your obedience to God is oftentimes a prerequisite for you to receive the favor of God. This widow's obedience in providing for Elijah's needs was definitely a factor in her son's life: Elijah was the first prophet recorded in the Bible to raise someone from the dead when her son fell sick (1 Kgs 17:22). This was a miracle that no amount of money could have bought. Your relationship with God can overcome all things, even death itself. This book is about building your wealth, but your relationship with God has to be the number one priority in your life. God has done a lot for you and He needs to get a return on His investment. Be an asset to your local church and local community, pay your tithes and offering on a consistent basis, purchase yourself a great study Bible with footnotes to grow deeper in the Word, read your study Bible, and attend service on a regular basis. Keep in mind that the leadership staff of your church is also human, and focus on being more of a blessing than a burden to them. The available balance in your account shouldn't determine your availability to God: God is your Lord and Savior not your ATM. Place yourself and your family in a position to make money, but keep yourself in position to hear from God.

# BLESSED BUT BROKE: BONUS CHALLENGE

"Write the vision and make it plain on tablets,
that he may run who reads it."
– Habakkuk 2:2

Thank you for completing this 60-day journey. I hope you have received information to strengthen your relationship with God and with your finances. Now it's time for action!

Write down your financial goals and the steps you will take to accomplish each one. Whether you want to save up to buy your first home, jump start your retirement savings, or pay off debt, there's no better time like the present to improve your financial future.

# BLESSED BUT BROKE: BONUS CHALLENGE

## Improve Your Health

Making all the money in the world is going to be pointless if you don't have the good health to enjoy it. If you don't already, find you a primary care physician.

- Once you have made contact with a physician, follow these steps:

- Schedule yourself a physical complete with blood work.

- Strategize ways to improve your physical condition.

- Commit yourself to a consistent workout regime.

- Implement more fruits and veggies into your diet.

I also recommend you get the book called *How Not To Die* by Michael Greger, M.D.

# LET'S CONNECT!

## SPEAKING REQUESTS

Darryl is available to host finance workshops and take speaking engagements for churches, financial conferences, business seminars, nonprofits, colleges, high schools, men's conferences, and youth groups. If you are interested in having him come to speak to your group, or if you'd like to share how this book has helped you, contact him at hello@darrylwboyles.com.

## PLEASE LEAVE A REVIEW

Thank you so much for your commitment to improve your finances by purchasing and reading this book. I sincerely hope you enjoyed it and found the information included valuable! I'd love to hear from you. Please leave a review on **Amazon** so you can help others learn how they can benefit from this book.

## ORDER YOUR COPY OF *ONE PAYCHECK AT TIME*

Does Money Have You Stressed Out?
In Darryl Boyles' debut book, One Paycheck at a Time, he reveals a powerful **step-by-step personal money management** system you can use to improve your finances even if you don't make enough, have too much debt, or don't know where to begin.

This is the book you'll WISH you had when you first became an adult. You'll discover practical, easy-to-apply ways to:

- **manage your money** like a boss (stress-free)
- **get good credit** (so you stop paying extra)
- **have more savings** (take peace of mind to the bank)
- **avoid common spending mistakes** (that are costing you thousands)
- **eliminate your debt fast** (no more being overwhelmed)

This book will jumpstart your journey to money mastery so you can **gain stability, better relationships, confidence, and peace of mind.**

Spend less time worrying about your money and more time enjoying your life and family by discovering simple, proven solutions to drastically improve your personal finances one paycheck at a time.

Order your copy today at onepaycheck.com or on Amazon.

# ABOUT THE AUTHOR

Darryl Boyles is a personal finance expert, speaker, author, and realtor.

A nationally-recognized Certified Financial Education Instructor, Darryl works to help his clients develop a healthy and powerful relationship with money. His latest work is the sequel to his debut best-selling book, *One Paycheck At A Time: Financial Solutions for Everyday People.*

He is the host of the show "Dollar Discussions," where he uses his own money story and experiences to empower men and women with relatable and proven financial strategies.

Darryl founded Bridge the Gap to help everyday people achieve their fullest potential through financial empowerment and entrepreneurship workshops, courses, and coaching.

He resides in Columbia, S.C. with his wife and children. To connect with Darryl, go to his website **darrylwboyles.com**.

Made in United States
Orlando, FL
05 November 2026

90230211R00121